Ecology
of Being

Published by All In All Books 2006
www.ecologyofbeing.com

Printed by Printing Arts Press, Mt. Vernon, Ohio
Standing Bear Image by John & Barbara King
Book design by Jerry Kelly
Printed in USA

ISBN 0-9777402-0-X

White, Peter, 1944 Nov. 11-
    Ecology of being / by Peter White.
        p. cm.
    ISBN 0-9777402-0-X
    1. Life.   I. Title.
BD431.W457 2006
128—dc22

                                        2006000920

Ecology
of Being

Peter White

All In All Books

Gambier, Ohio
New York
2006

Contents

Preface

What does it mean to be human? How does the quality of being human influence the quality of the world? What gives quality to being human?

Ecology of Being describes how human nature, purpose and destiny relate to the quality of existence. It explains not what to do but how to be. It offers a context for understanding the immense implications of being.

The intended audience for the book is busy, educated people — people who are interested in meeting needs and reaching goals: the kind of people who don't want to deal with abstractions but prefer information that seems concrete and immediately helpful. *Ecology of Being* is not, in current business parlance, demand-driven. I do not know what specific steps readers should take to have better relationships or become more effective leaders or achieve exceptional results in their careers.

Why should people who are deeply concerned with such things engage themselves in a subject so *out there* as the nature and quality of existence?

The overwhelming desire for concrete information is evident everywhere. Best-sellers advise us on getting into prestigious colleges, building beautiful bodies, winning in business, retiring with money to spare, and staying young and alive indefinitely. They explain how to find release from addiction and how to have successful relationships. They tell us how to move quickly, to multitask, and to seek answers we can use right now. They describe the frightening state of the world — stirring up more fear, assigning blame and confidently prescribing remedies. In a multitude of genres and from an infinity of angles, they tell us who we are. The flood of publications about such things reveals the intense struggle that is contemporary life.

That the flood flows and the demand does not ebb also tells us that our popular literature isn't working. I don't mean to be flippant: many books and magazines offer interesting observations and sound advice. But despite all the how-to advice in the abundant marketplace, we are still in the wilderness, working too hard, eating too much and searching unsuccessfully for love. The world becomes more fragile and chaotic and we are depressed by the portents of disaster. We are self-conscious to a point of obsession, but self-identity remains elusive.

Something more than concrete detail is required.

We think and act within the framework of our underlying beliefs — the operating software of how we live and experience life. The failure to solve our individual and collective problems by trying to do things differently reflects not a lack of specific information but the limitations of the assumptions underlying our busy, well-informed lives.

The assumptions that determine how we feel and what we think and do prevent us from assessing and changing how we feel and what we think and do. They blind us and bind us. Real change requires more than resolving to feel, think and act differently, more than information about new approaches, more even than good counsel and inspiration. To change our conscious lives we must change our unconscious assumptions. We must free ourselves from the belief systems that limit us.

How can we let go of something so fundamental as the assumptions that shape our experience? How can we go beyond ourselves?

One way is to learn and grow when life deprives us of what we assume to be essential. We lose our job, our beloved leaves us for someone else, our health fails, a parent or a child dies, someone we admire is revealed as a fraud — our basic beliefs are shaken by disaster and we must either give up or accept and grow. But we can also grow without having to endure painful loss.

Readers who are prepared to set aside their desire for techniques and data can find within their intuitive knowledge a new sense of truth. Finding this truth provides room to stretch beyond limiting belief systems and abandon self-defeating assumptions. This means that we must let go of the illusion that truth may be found in the timeful world and put our faith in the essentials, the great and everlasting abstractions: meaning, freedom, love and unity. These are what we find when we are willing to explore what it means to be human, how the quality of being human influences the quality of the world, and what gives quality to being human.

How do I know what I'm talking about? *Ecology of Being* is based on lessons learned in sorting out a complicated life and on sources relied upon in the process, including ancient wisdom and more recent science and philosophy. But the principal source is my own experience.

My life today is centered upon solitude and practices of the spirit; yet I am also a father, friend and adviser to people very much in the world. Therefore, I am also of the world and fully complicit in human thought and action. How were these two contrary tracks laid for the passage of a single life?

Thirty-three years ago I was an ambitious young lawyer in Washington, D.C., working for an important law firm on the Watergate case. My role was as a junior member of a legal team, but I went to court with the senior lawyers and felt the thrill of flashing cameras and reporters thrusting microphones and shouting out questions. Shortly after Watergate was over I became the government's chief counsel in its antitrust suit to restructure the petroleum industry, the largest case of its kind ever brought. I left the government in 1975 and became a partner in the law firm of Fulbright & Jaworski, headed by Leon Jaworski, the former Watergate prosecutor. By the early 1980s I had a soaring career, a picture-perfect family, a fine house, money, reputation and recognition in my profession and a place in Washington society.

Things were great, but I had a problem.

Below the glittering surface I experienced a dark emptiness, which left me confused and anxious.

What was I really trying to accomplish? Where was I going? What mattered to me? What, if anything, did I believe in? I don't believe I could have said.

I had everything but was afraid I would lose it. Accomplishing something meant focusing on it and throwing all my energy into it, but when success came the experience felt hollow. I moved on quickly to the next challenge. I wasn't sleeping soundly, I had headaches, I felt anxious about the future and guilty about the past. I expected to find *enough* over the next mountain peak of accomplishment, but when I got there I saw only another peak to surmount.

Nothing was enough. As my experience was inevitably unsatisfactory, I abandoned people, moved to new places and obtained new jobs, thinking I would find satisfaction if circumstances were different. I was as blind as Oedipus wandering about the world. But I was not blind to the world — I had the world well fixed in my sight. I was blind to myself.

As a child I had been introspective, curious about myself and the nature of things. I

loved candy but ate it and it was gone.
What did it bring me while it was here?
Enjoyment. What was enjoyment? What
was enjoyment when it ended? What was
its purpose then and its value now? When I
ate candy and realized it would soon be
gone, I tried to observe the benefit while I
still had it in my mouth. Somehow my
awareness that it would soon be gone made
the tasting seem pointless. How could
something that ended mean anything?

I fantasized much. I imagined that I
was like my cowboy heroes, Hopalong
Cassidy and the Lone Ranger, thwarting
bad guys and saving damsels. I noticed
that instead of resolving themselves, my
fantasies went on and on. I didn't want
them to end because after a story ended,
what did you have? Emptiness. The story
had to conclude to mean something, but
when it did it was like swallowed candy.
The ending of the fantasy seemed to give it
meaning — grateful townspeople, adoring
girl — but actually took the excitement
away, leaving emptiness.

I was intrigued by ambiguity. I thought
about how measurement was impossible
because no matter how minutely you measured — whether in fractions of inches or

fractions of seconds — the measurement could never be exactly right. Inches can be broken down indefinitely and time is always moving. I tried to imagine the end of the universe. How could it end? If the end of the universe was a wall, it had to have thickness and therefore it was not the end of the universe. The thickness was. And what was behind that? I believed that if the universe went on forever, it was certain that someone was out there exactly like me, thinking exactly as I was.

Almost every night as I lay in bed before I went to sleep, my mind followed a path to the idea of death and not-existing. Someday there will be no Peter White! That inconceivable conception terrified me until I shook myself or got out of bed for a drink of water. Who would I be when I wasn't anyone? Between now and then how could my life make any difference? Would my life be like a piece of candy?

No doubt many children experience such terrors. Death issues to the young a merciless invitation to begin the consideration of a lifetime: given death, what does life mean?

Those fears and enigmas affected me half a century ago. I was born in 1944. My father was a physician and a decorated veteran of World War II, and my mother was a pleasing and pretty young woman. We lived in the suburbs of a great industrial city. I remember how cocky and purposeful my parents and their friends were in those sunny postwar days. They had survived the Great Depression and won the War; in the aftermath of deprivation and upheaval they shared a dream of prosperity and order.

America had emerged predominant in the world. But as I look back I can see that with the disruptions of World War II, the Depression and social upheaval, we had lost our internal compass. On the surface we appeared confident; below the surface we were shaky and anxious. As the controlled 1950s gave way to the chaotic 1960s, the question for me and my contemporaries was where did we belong? Many clung to the postwar ideal of an ordered world; many caught in the tumult of the sixties rebelled. I clung to the norms of the postwar era and pursued success single-mindedly. I went to college and law school, did well, and dived into my striving years desperate for the world to define and affirm me.

A ferocious desire to create myself in the eyes of others launched my law career like rocket fuel. My talent, drive and bravado propelled my ascent to the pinnacles, but when I looked at where I was standing, the height terrified me and I loathed my inadequacy. I was afraid of falling and I wanted to jump. I had an acute awareness of what was expected of me and no idea of who I was. My values were whatever I perceived in the eyes of those who beheld me.

The turmoil inside made the experience hard to endure. I did my best to fit marriage, fatherhood and friendship between two ephemeral pillars, working and drinking. I moved between exemplary accomplishment by day and a secret life of nocturnal alcoholic binges, trying by night to find relief from the day's fear and self-loathing.

I had long forgotten the questions that intrigued me as a boy. In 1981, when I began to look realistically at myself, processes began unfolding that brought me back and made me face them. Life stripped away the veneer I had applied.

A new way of life in a community of people dealing with addiction to alcohol and drugs led me away from the achievement-centered mindset of upper middle-class culture. Almost every decision I had made became unmade and the unions I had formed were broken. I left the practice of law. I divorced and broke up my family, remarried and divorced again. My ability to endure these changes while attempting to discharge my responsibilities as father, husband and professional came from support and wisdom tendered by many who appeared, in groups, as mentors and teachers, friends and voices from the ages.

Others around me had to endure as much or more than I did in the winding up and down of my life. The suffering I caused them is the one thing I regret. I acknowledge this with sorrow.

Loss forced me to understand the lesson and virtue of detachment: what I cling to as if it were crucial to my wellbeing is usually quite dispensable and letting go of what I desire most provides an opening to freedom.

In 1986, when I left the practice of law, I started my own business and consulting firm, International Skye. I began working with charities, helping them become more effective as businesses in the competitive environment of the Reagan years. I became an official with one of my clients, Hazelden Foundation, the pioneering center in Minnesota for rehabilitating alcoholics and drug addicts. Hazelden's approach to recovery was based upon caring community. Hazelden's ability to bring back to life people who would otherwise have been hopeless cases abandoned in "drying out" sanitariums and on skid row, affected me profoundly.

What I also absorbed at Hazelden, unconsciously at least, was the idea that I could integrate my personal intellectual and spiritual journey with my work. Later on I perceived a business opportunity when I began unexpectedly getting to know people who had amassed or inherited great wealth. I could see that the problem of a life of extraordinary abundance was essentially the same as the problem of alcoholism. One can possess the riches of Midas yet remain mired in meaninglessness and self-destruction. I found a profession in offering community and detachment as responses to the seemingly practical problems of inheritance, family legacy and family business succession, and resolving family conflicts about business and money.

The wealthy, who have so many avenues of escape, responded surprisingly well. By the early 1990s I was working as a teacher, facilitator, mentor and organizer of workshops and service projects whose final purpose was to help people release their grasp upon the world and find themselves and each other within.

In the intervening years I have been a university professor teaching ethics and family enterprise. I have served as a mentor to men and women seeking answers to problems that seem practical — relationships, careers, dealing with parents, raising children, among others — but are deeply spiritual. My work today is teaching and learning about the spirit in the realm of material abundance.

My professional work is with people, but the work that is crucial to my search for deeper meaning is done alone. In solitude I concentrate on practices of the spirit: meditation and contemplation. I seek to attain focus and discipline. I seek myself.

Order is emerging from a chaotic life because of gifts: an early curiosity about what is essential, an intuitive eye, detachment earned from loss and spiritual practice, healing in community, the stern and loving integrity of mentors, wisdom from the ages and from modern science and philosophy, and time to assimilate, teach and learn. What I have learned is distilled and organized here.

My objective is to paint for busy but thoughtful readers a portrait of existence, using common words and as few of them as possible. I hope to give readers an insight that will help them find freedom from assumptions that bind them to feelings and thought and action that do not serve them or the world well.

This is a large ambition for a small book, requiring a valid offering from me and a willingness from you to allow *Ecology of Being* to register intuitively. I suggest that you read slowly, reflectively, inquisitively and imaginatively, and that you do your best to suspend reflexive disbelief and assess as open-mindedly as you can. In the brief experience of reading this book, allow it to take you to a different place from which to view the scene.

You may find support for understanding *Ecology of Being* on the website www.ecologyofbeing.com, and you may use the site to ask me questions and offer your own ideas and reflections.

Whether in *Ecology of Being* or at ecol-ogyofbeing.com or somewhere else in the ecology of being, I know I will be in touch with you.

P.W.
November 2005

Introduction

Mystery

Mystery presents an anomaly, a departure from the logic we prize. We are inclined to dismiss it. But even as mystery troubles our analytic, results-oriented minds, it awakens something within and beckons us to learn.

The story I am about to relate registers with me as mystery. I learned it long ago, and over the years, as I have told it many times, it has changed, evolving into the story presented here. But its mysterious essence has remained the same.

Many years ago and far away, an aged teacher was strolling contemplatively in the corridor of the dormitory that housed the students of his academy. As he passed the doorway of an especially favored student, he noticed that the young man was preparing for a journey. "Where are you going?" the teacher asked.

"Master, I have heard there is a vicious warlord in a region far from here who is oppressing the people, stealing their land, taxing them into poverty and enriching himself while they starve. I have prepared myself for mortal combat and I am going to this region, where I intend to force the warlord to cease his outrageous conduct."

Instead of being impressed, as the disciple had hoped, the teacher laughed derisively. "He will brush you away with the back of his hand. You will accomplish nothing but getting yourself killed."

Perplexed, the student thought for a moment. "I know! I will use the power of reason, which I have learned from you, to convince the warlord that his violent ways can only result in an uprising of the people and the overthrow of his regime. Surely reason will prevail!"

Again the master laughed at his well-intentioned disciple. "Your reason will be as effective as reasoning with a river to reverse its course. You will drown!"

Frustrated but ever anxious to find the right answer, the student meditated.

Suddenly he smiled and returned to his master's gaze. "I believe I see what you are saying, my esteemed teacher. I must invoke a force greater than my physical strength and my logic to make this wretched man mend his ways. I must invoke the power of God, showing the warlord that God despises the greedy and violent and will surely impose a punishment greater by a thousand times than the material rewards the warlord receives from his oppression."

"Ha, ha, ha!" the old man nearly doubled over in laughter, "The thought of you invoking God, threatening to bring lightning bolts down upon this ruler! Your only hope is that the ridiculous nature of your posturing will move him to ignore you."

Deflated as he had never been before, the student pondered once again, and then spoke. "I have it! I will forget force, forget reason, forget even God, and I will go in rags as a beggar. In the mirror of my humility, the warlord will see himself as he truly is and will decide on his own to change his violent ways."

"He will swat you away as an irrelevant insect!" came the master's response, again with derisive laughter.

The student was exasperated. Burning tears flowed down his cheeks and sputtered from his lips, as he cried, "Master, you yourself have said repeatedly that behavior like that of this warlord is wrong and cannot be countenanced. I have committed myself to putting an end to the injustice, to laying down my life if necessary. I have described the best plans I can devise, and you only belittle me and laugh at me. Tell me, please, Master, what must I do?"

"You must fast."

The first time I heard this story it didn't suit my logical mind but pricked my intuition and beckoned me almost playfully to learn.[1] I find it a good place to start looking not only at our world but at how we are looking at our world.

The steepness and stubbornness of the world's decline call into question the future of humanity itself. Everywhere, violence menaces humankind as a present reality or as an imminent possibility. The increasing separation between rich and poor both demoralizes people and inflames their hostile passions. The technology of destruction is evolving and spreading. With humanity in a violent frame of mind, the prospects for peace are poor.

At the same time, we are stripping the earth of essential resources, disrupting the ecosystems that sustain our lives. We know that the earth is an organism of which human beings are prominently and indivisibly part. But the more we injure ourselves in this way, the more we feel the need to plunder and damage the earth, or ourselves.

We have nearly obliterated silence. Words, which depend on silence, are losing their meaning. We are deafened and muted by these losses. The experience of beauty and

[1] The story that inspired this story is called "The Fasting of the Heart," which may be found in *The Way of Chuang Tzu* by Thomas Merton, New Directions (1965).

delight is slipping away and we are dispirited. As the spirit fades we raise the level of noise and seek solace in having and doing, which ties back into violence and waste.

Our helplessness and confusion keep us in a state of fear — not necessarily fear of something specific but a general dread or anxiety in which we interpret almost everything as a threat. This fear leads us to ways of thinking and doing that produce fear in others, who then act in ways that make us afraid. Fear yields fear.

These phenomena are self-perpetuating and interrelated. When you look carefully at one problem, you see other problems feeding into it and you see it feeding back into them. The elements of the decline cause decline in themselves and each other. The human being is both a cause and an effect in the process. Objective things and subjective experience entwine in a double helix of mutual dependence.

In a way there is nothing new in this. Civilizations rise, begin to prosper, flourish and then spin out of control, fade away or are demolished by other civilizations. Rise and fall is an old story and we have survived as a species even though massive numbers of people have suffered in the process.

What is different now is that we have run out of room. The explosion of technology and population has left nowhere to go. The interdependence and proximity of systems which are life and upon which life depends make us vulnerable to ourselves as never before. Existence as a unity is not only a religious or philosophical concept but a practical fact. Our ability, or willingness, to adapt to that reality is both crucial and in doubt.

On the other hand, reversal of the vicious cycle of human existence is conceivable.

Innovations in science and technology have made it possible to accommodate the survival needs of the swelling population. The earth's resources are probably sufficient, if managed carefully, to provide for its human inhabitants over the long run.

We travel and communicate with each other as if the entire world were our home. This interconnectedness, which makes us vulnerable, also creates the ground for a common effort to address our problems.

The will to find meaning is far from extinct. Neither learning nor the creation of beauty have disappeared. The spirit just wants inspiration to enable it to do its work of inspiring.

As for genocide, war and terrorism, a

child could prescribe the solution: we need only treat others as we would like to be treated.

Full of hope and indignation, we rush in to solve problems. Our tools — scientific, economic, military, political, philanthropic — are impressive and we have the will to match. Still our efforts do not reverse the deteriorating situation.

Instead the results we achieve tend to fall along the lines of those the master predicted for his well-intentioned disciple.

Perhaps we must fast.

Part I
Ecology of Being

Systems

I cannot think of any phenomenon that has no systemic involvement. Literally, there is none — from whirling galaxies containing billions of stars billions of light years away from earth, held in pattern by each other's gravity, to electrons whirling around the nucleus of an atom, held in pattern by the strong nuclear force.

An organizing principle is at work forming patterns. Ant colonies function efficiently in patterns emerging from a few basic signals. In the narrow tunnels and cramped walkways of the New York City subway, millions of people filter into, around and back out of the city in a single work day. Wandering alone in forests and fields can be bewildering, but from an airplane the same places appear in recognizable geometric patterns, making sense *en masse*. My life seems pointless and chaotic until years later I look back and see a coherent pattern — a story.

The lines in an old weathered face. A well-ordered French garden, a disorderly English one, a serene Japanese garden with water tumbling from rock to rock. Young players in a string quartet begin playing self-consciously, then lose themselves in the music. We find patterns whether they are obvious or disguised or subtle. A double play from short to second to first. A fluttery new friendship, an unconscious old one.

Patterns are mysterious and beautiful, conducive to awe and delight. Their beauty and mystery call us persistently to an awareness of relationship.

Human beings are composed of miniscule particles operating in relation to one another. Patterns attract the human eye and heart because they appeal to the essence of human existence.

The atom is a system of positively and negatively charged thinglets spinning around and around each other, chaotically in parts but as a whole in relationship, exerting pushing or pulling influences and forming discernible patterns. The interaction creates stability so that the atom can take its place as the heart of physical matter. The atom — the essential unit of physical being — is a system.

Relationship gives the inert particles their meaning and function. In a sense the atom is alive because it sustains itself in forces pulling and pushing its parts, creating a whole. If you think of it as a living thing, you would say it wants to survive. It derives its character and identity — its meaning — from the systemic nature of its being. The whole exists, survives and takes on meaning because of the relationship among its parts.

The systemic nature of the atom sets the stage for the nature of all physical reality.

Physics turns into chemistry as atoms cluster together in various ways to compose themselves as molecules. As molecules join together at a more complex level of systems, they become elements of matter, in relationship, exerting positive and negative forces on one another that create chemical bonds. Molecules and elements, like atoms, are unconscious but alive in the sense of being in relationship, deriving meaning from relationship and seeking to remain in relationship.

In biology we have cells made up of chemical elements operating in relation to one another. Biological cells change. They split and grow, age and die. They sustain themselves through closed, internal interaction and by open, external relations with their environs. They acquire nourishment and expel waste; they contain themselves and repel invaders. Cells and molecules are in a holding pattern, but the pattern shifts: change takes place.

Animals are systems of systems of systems — collections of organs made of cells, connected by organic tubing and structural material and wrapped in a complex organ called skin. Human beings are complex systems, our components interdependent, in constant change, in a pattern of sameness, seeking to maintain the basic pattern despite the change. If one part of the system breaks down, another tries to replace it, to keep the balance and maintain the living pattern.

What defines a system is the interdependence of its parts and its will — to keep functioning, to stabilize itself, to support the other components, to coerce them to carry on in whatever role they play.

In an ecosystem the components behave in ways which hold the whole ensemble together and keep it moving forward toward its goal or destiny. Plants, animals, air, water and earth combine to keep each other alive and flourishing. The ecosystem will live indefinitely if it isn't thwarted by the degradation of critical elements. And if an imbalance or disruption occurs, the system may find a way to heal itself, with one part growing or diminishing to restore equilibrium or taking over the function of the impaired part. Dead pine needles on the forest floor choke out new growth. They become the fuel for a fire that destroys the decaying forest and sets the stage for renewal.

Never am I more content in a particular place than when I am in Yellowstone Park, where I worked during summers in college. I fell in love in Yellowstone then — with people, with fun and adventure, and with the wilderness. Now as an older man I return to Yellowstone for recollection and renewal.

Yellowstone was the first national park in the world and is still one of the largest. It is roughly in the shape of a square with its four sides measuring about sixty miles each. The Park contains a splendid array of natural phenomena, from lakes and rivers and streams to boiling hot pools and geysers great and small, from grasses to giant pine trees, from mosquitoes to moose. What you learn in Yellowstone if you pay attention is how the natural elements simultaneously attack and support one another. The atmosphere provides both life-giving rain and lightning that starts forest fires. The predation of hunters like wolves thins animal populations, allowing the herds to prosper.

All in all, the natural phenomena of Yellowstone achieve a dynamic balance. Naturalists look at this balance holistically, in terms of systems. Ecosystems are natural elements interacting to form an integrated complex of mutual dependence. Out of the giving and taking that goes on constantly within ecosystems comes sustained life.

Of course, if a wilderness area is made into a park, nature must bend to human accommodation. Since the establishment of Yellowstone National Park in 1872, the United States government has been seeking to achieve the right balance between human activity and the ebb and flow of natural systems. A great deal of the talk that goes on among officials and employees in Yellowstone concerns this delicate equation.

Not only do disturbances to the systemic balance within the Park create problems, but changes in the natural environment hundreds of miles outside Yellowstone have a direct impact. New housing in the sur rounding valleys affects the animal populations and migrations, which subsequently affect the plant life and air quality, which in turn play back into the area's flora and fauna and even change the nutrient content of water in its aquifers, lakes and rivers. Yellowstone contains the headwaters for three great river systems, which infuse the Park back into the nation. The real ecosystem of Yellowstone Park extends well beyond its borders.

Even the systems of the global environment impact the Park's systemic environment. The macro-ecosystem of Yellowstone reaches outside the United States. As rain forests vanish from Central and South America, levels of carbon dioxide increase around the globe, which impedes the growth of new forests in Yellowstone.

A system is by definition a relationship or a web of relationships where everything influences everything else. "Pull a string on one end of that web and you will find it attached to everything else."[2]

Systems entered my consciousness in Yellowstone Park.

A hurricane emerges when low-pressure weather systems coincide over tropical ocean waters, combining to form a single swarm of air and water, sucking up warm water from the ocean to fuel the swirling mass. As the mass increases, more warm water is drawn up for energy and the mass

[2] Greater Yellowstone Coalition, www.greateryellowstone.org

increases, drawing up more water and so on. Thus the hurricane sustains itself. We give it a human name. Hurricane systems dissipate when they move over land or north to cooler waters and spend their energy without a source for replenishment.

Patterns of energy accumulation and dissipation occur also in the human realm. The act of conception, with its mutual surges of energy drawing and yielding floods of spermatozoa to engage the waiting egg, is itself a dramatic system that portends the cycle of life it puts in play. Our own bodies form in the womb as cells coming together in muscle and bone structures, vessels and organs, which then function as more complex systems – digestive, respiratory, muscular, cardiovascular and nervous. The body is a system made of interdependent subsystems. As the decades pass the systems of physical being proceed toward their inevitable breakdown. Finally we die.

The mystery of consciousness itself can be explained in terms of highly evolved sensory systems. Years ago there was a child's toy in which vertical mirrors were erected like a solid picket fence around a small circular platform with clowns and animal figurines. When the mirrors were still, they reflected broken images of the figures. But by making the mirrors whirl around the platform at a particular velocity, the reflected images of the figures appeared to be moving vividly in three dimensions. This is how I understand consciousness.

People are complex systems that include the mystery of consciousness and they participate with each other through relationship. A friendship is a system in which two people, however casually or intensely, become something together that is greater than the sum of their parts. Here we see systemic relatedness in its spiritual — nonphysical — dimension: a connection no less real than that of atoms, molecules, elements and cells.

When we see a person we love or someone we have loved, we experience a quickened heartbeat, an involuntary smile, a spring in the step, a blush. These physical responses confirm the spiritual reality of relationship. Relationships engrave patterns in our conscious minds and also in the unconscious mind. These patterns form the architecture of new relationships.

Family is now understood systemically. We grow up, go out in the world and become autonomous people with our own identities. Or so we think, until we "go home" to visit our parents and feel like we are ten years old again. We may hear, "You look well today," or "I think you're a few minutes late," in our daily lives with minimal effect. But in our families the implied meanings can be explosive, evoking feelings and provoking responses unimaginable elsewhere. These phrases send signals to us below the level of consciousness because of their meanings in the family system. It is difficult to see these patterns from within the family system, but after separating, the power of familial relations becomes evident.

A family is a system and a system is like a family: you can walk away but you can never resign from it and forget it. It stays a part of you and you stay a part of it.

Tension holds systems in place. The solar system is held in place by the tension among its components created by gravitational forces pulling in opposite directions. The life of cells is maintained by the outer membranes acting as an opening for receiving nutrition and expelling waste and as a blockade against the ingress of poisons and the escape of vital substances. Adjusting that tension to get it right over time maintains life.

All systems are to some extent open and to some extent closed, and there is a tension between them. Too open, the system disintegrates; too closed, it collapses. The ability of systems to open and close according to the needs of the moment determines their ability to survive in the long run. A cell must be open to nutrients and closed against hostile invaders. Parenthood is a balancing act between control and letting go. Businesses must consider both their profit motive and their communal obligations. Charities balance their idealism against economic reality. Religions must be open to new participants without abandoning their principles. Nations must secure their borders while remaining open to trade. The vitality of a system depends on how well these opposing elements maintain each other in fluid equipoise.

Systems connect and empower, but this connectedness also creates a poignant vulnerability. A tree rubs against electric wires in Ohio and power shuts down throughout the northeastern United States and southeastern Canada. A computer hacker threatens the global communication system. Cancer invades a single organ, sapping the strength of the entire body.

Systemic balance is both delicate and obstinate. Disruption can be relatively easy but systems have a way of reasserting themselves. Intervening or imposing change on systems is hard because of their self-generating, reinforcing nature. Whatever we change in one place will cause a corresponding change elsewhere to restore the system's equilibrium.

Ecological obstinacy — the innate will of the natural environment to survive — enables ecosystems to endure devastating blows from human incursion. Underground communication networks remain intact despite the interventions of repressive regimes. Information and transportation systems are reestablished after terrorist attacks. People who are sick or injured live on through sheer willpower even though their bodies have seriously deteriorated.

When human beings become involved in systems all the dimensions of consciousness come into play. Thought in its broadest sense — from emotion to intellect and from intuition to will — becomes a component in the system. The way one thinks and discerns is what designs the system and maintains it, and the system in turn shapes the way the individual thinks and discerns.

Because systems maintain themselves it is inadequate to regard any one component as an isolated cause or effect. Every component of a system is a cause *and* an effect.

Systems exist at the core of nature as atoms and extend into the limitlessness of nature as galaxies. Human beings are systems made up of systems and function as parts of the complex of systems that comprise our social and physical environment: Cells, infants, parents and children, siblings, mothers and fathers, grandparents, families, friends, enemies, lovers, flowers, crops, hives, orchards, farms, forests, mammals, birds, fish, insects, bacteria, viruses, algae, aquifers, rivers, lakes and oceans, bays and harbors, tide pools, swamps, mud, dust, fog, smoke, ore, fuel, factories, warehouses, offices, businesses, markets, industries, towns, cities, governments, nations, the United Nations, rich people, poor people, the middle class, dropouts and outcasts, celebrities, intellectuals, laborers, achievers, activists, soldiers, politicians, polemicists, teachers, gardeners, doctors, schools, universities, charities, religions, cultures, civilizations, atmosphere and space, moons and planets, galaxies and stars, those who are dying and those who are about to be born.

Science is exploring the potentially infinite reaches of the universe and the infinitesimal elements of being itself. These searches will not end in a conclusive discovery. The scientist seeking the infinite will run smack dab into the one seeking the infinitesimal.

Human Systems

What is purely natural — untouched by people — is without positive or negative value. A wilderness ecosystem simply exists; it is neither good nor bad. What gives systems their moral quality is the human element. In addition to their basic circularity as systems, human systems ascend or decline in a qualitative way. Personal relationships, families, professional associations, governments — systems whose components are human beings — function for better or for worse. Over time, with temporary fluctuations up and down, alongside periods of relative equilibrium, their quality ascends or declines.

The element of human influence adds moral quality to systems that otherwise would be neutral. Human beings erect cathedrals and human beings destroy ecosystems. A city is built on a natural site out of materials derived from nature. But as you survey a city you can see human elements that deride quality, like drugs and violence, and those that enhance it, such as universities and charities.

Human systems take on qualitative

momentum and tend to maintain their qualitative directions. Moral quality produces moral quality. Kindness induces kindness. Violence leads to violence. A stimulus motivates a response in kind, often one that exceeds the stimulus. A person or a nation struck violently responds with greater violence. A single act of charity moves greater numbers of people to give and serve.

Moral improvement — a system ascending as a spiral — is a rarer and more vulnerable phenomenon than a system in descent. Declining spirals maintain their momentum or accelerate absent extraordinary intervention. We see declining spirals in physics, as when we observe water flowing from a bowl down a drain. After it begins to flow, a whirlpool develops and the flow increases the whirlpool effect, which increases the flow, and so on.

The idea of ascending spirals pleases the imagination. Fireworks display upward spirals. I remember from childhood a mesmerizing toy that had a round metal plate with a spiral like design. By using a plunger you could make the plate spin faster and faster, creating the impression of spiraling flight. Barber's poles create a similar impression as the painted spiral appears to ascend forever. A whirling water sprinkler catches the eye. Fugues and rondos are ascending spirals in music.

In nature declining spirals are real and ascending spirals are flights of fancy. Human beings have a special ability to make flights of fancy come true. Relationships like long-standing marriages can be ascending spirals over time. Families can remain strong and vibrant. Any human association can be an ascending spiral depending on the quality of the relationship.

Within human systems an ascending spiral like a growing friendship requires work, as if to pull against gravity. One friend does something kind for another and this creates a safe space and the motivation for a kindness in return. But what if the recipient sees the kindness as a trap? What if the person performing the kindness has been unkind in the past? The recipient must choose whether to overcome his suspicion and accept the favor, or to reject it, winging the spiral in the beginning of its potential ascent.

If the first friend is sincere and if the recipient decides to trust and forgive, the spiral will continue to ascend. If he yields to his suspicion or resentment, the spiral will likely turn toward decline.

Love elevates systems, causing them to ascend as spirals and to evolve creatively in their ascension. Fear causes systems to decline. Fear is to human existence as gravity is to physical objects, unyielding. Love can defeat fear as a rocket can defeat gravity, but love, unlike fear, requires a moral effort of gravity-defeating intensity.

Human systems in ascension easily lose their momentum and revert to decline. There is far more reversal of spirals from ascension to decline than from decline to ascension. It is easier to turn a good system to bad than a bad one to good. To understand this we must look at love and fear, the fuels for ascension and decline in human systems.

Love elevates human systems. When I speak of love I refer to far more than affection or caring deeply for another person. I am describing devotion to principle — something one cannot possess — and unselfish thought and action that create. Doing the hard, uncertain, dangerous work of overcoming natural fear is love.

We must understand love in terms of devotion to an ideal, working against inertia and entropy. This devotion exists not only in the relationships of friends and lovers, the usual settings for considerations of love, but in all of human life.

For example, it takes devotion to develop a talent. One must have the desire to learn, the humility to emulate and the discipline to practice. Love is doing the hard, practical work of turning a talent into an art.

Love is the effort of scientists who spend careers trying to discover or develop something they believe in when they cannot know what the result of their work will be.

Giving up worldly things to serve the cause of the spirit is love.

Comforting someone who is behaving obnoxiously is love. Understanding without needing to be understood is also love.

Creating community, in which people acting together exceed the sum of their individual capabilities, is leadership as love.

The peacemaker who inspires others to lay down their weapons acts in love.

The person who relinquishes precious property in order to benefit others acts in love. The devotion that love requires can motivate extreme sacrifice, as when a mother gives up life so that her child may live, or when a soldier dies while doing his duty.

Love brings virtue, such as loyalty, commitment, discipline, authenticity, compassion and caring, to thought and action. Love is a force against inertia, and this creative element is what causes human systems to ascend.

Love is a universal force but the realization of love depends on human beings. With a willed exertion that itself is love, human beings can tap into the force of love and rise above themselves and raise the world above itself.

Fear causes decline.

Fear brings about what it wants to avoid. A jealous, controlling person drives his partner to infidelity whether or not there was ground for suspicion in the first place. Fear of scarcity deprives people of the experience of enough, urging them to excess, whirling the meaning out of their lives and ultimately bankrupting them. Imperialism and tyranny bring about their own destruction.

Fear, like love, is more than an emotion: it is a way of knowing. Fear arises from a sense of helplessness. Fear assumes the worst. Fear leads people to reject love, often when they need it most. Fear is a condition of anxiety and discomfort in the spirit, an attitude that leads to diminishing thought and action.

Fear can be useful when it alerts us to an immediate threat. But most of the time, as privileged citizens of the developed world, the danger exists not in external circumstances but in the fearful lens through which we see. Because fear creates fear, the greatest danger is fear.

Fear is present from birth to compel us to survive. Fear comes first and we return to it reflexively. Love is the spirit to which humankind may aspire, but fear is the condition to which we tend strongly to revert under pressure. Systems move more easily from ascension to decline than from decline to ascension because fear is the baseline condition of life.

Qualitative direction perpetuates qualitative direction.

People in vibrant relationships work to preserve them and protect them against intrusion. Friends and lovers care and accommodate, as do family members who want to cultivate and protect family unity. Members of successful athletic teams, professional firms, charities or businesses commit to a vision and to each other. A young democracy thrives on the dynamic tension among national purpose, a government with constitutionally separated powers and a free, informed electorate. The United Nations was born in recognition of common international interests while respecting national sovereignty.

Declining quality tends strongly to perpetuate decline. In fear friends and lovers, families, organizations of every kind, nations and groups of nations, defeat themselves.

In decline fearful human beings preserve and increase what they do not want. Resistance to change is the hallmark of declining systems. In decline people diminish themselves and fragment communities. We see this in self-destructive individuals, in abusive marriages and among nations that, locked in blind animosity, threaten to suck the entire world into a hateful vortex.

Human influence pervades and dominates the infinity of interacting and interconnected systems that comprise existence. Love and fear are in conflict throughout the systemic unity.

As in individual and family lives, breakdowns occur in organizations that take them off their course, sending them in a disastrous direction. People whose work began with a shared vision become afraid, losing track of what they wanted to accomplish. As people begin to suspect the worst in each other, everyone's actions are perceived in ways that confirm the suspicions. Mutual commitments are abandoned and people act as adversaries instead of allies. A divisive pattern is established and grooves itself onto the collective psyche of the group, which then imprints itself on the psyches of the individuals, who think and act in ways that feed back to the group. Ultimately the organization disintegrates, torn apart by internal power struggles that have nothing to do with the originating ideas and principles.

Fear has created a pervasive, geometric decline in responsibility across the globe. There is a growing economic disparity between the consuming industrialized world and the suffering non-industrialized world. In regions of overwhelming poverty the property-rich few aggrandize while the masses of the poor sink into misery. In the wealthy regions a well-educated, aggressive overclass separates from an uninformed, despairing, angry underclass.

As the divisions increase so does the level of irresponsibility. Wealthy nations neglect poorer nations and the poor nations recede or provoke. Oligarchs in the unindustrialized world aggrandize and tyrannize, isolating themselves while the poor recede and provoke. In the industrialized world ambitious people gain wealth, power and celebrity, and the disadvantaged recede and provoke.

The common element among these polarizing phenomena is a decreasing sense of relationship to the whole. Separation leads to separating thought and action and the downward spiral continues.

In a world of human predomination the essential, subtle and unacknowledged problem is that you and I belong to these systems. The failure to understand and own our indivisibility leads humankind to a crucial, hubristic fallacy. We persist in the illusion that root causes exist outside ourselves and that we and institutions we create can identify and ameliorate these root causes without attending to our own responsibility for them.

Our efforts to change the world are like trying to reverse the spin of a carousel by standing on the platform and pushing against one of the horses.

Conversation

If systems are completely open they will dissipate; if they are completely closed they will collapse. Creative, evolving systems depend upon opening and closing forces working together, in *conversation*. The conversation between opening and closing values is crucial to the quality of systems and to their duration.

In the case of atoms the strong nuclear force holds the electrons in orbit around the nuclei. Without that closing force the electrons would spin off into eternity, sucked into chaos by external forces. Without the balancing influence of those external forces, however, the nuclear force would suck the orbiting electrons into the nuclei and the whole enterprise would collapse.

The nuclear force of atoms is akin to gravity's holding the planets in fluid equipoise as they rotate around the sun: a closing, organizing force conversing with an opening, chaotically-inclined force. Too much organization leads to collapse, too little results in dissipation.

In human systems conversation is no less crucial than in systems of nature. The conversation is always seeking (because it never quite finds) a balance that stabilizes the system. Friendship requires the opening value of communication revealing personality: what a person thinks and feels, wants and fears, believes and doubts. But there are limits. The relationship must be contained, as skin contains the physical body. Few friendships can survive total communication. What is revealed must include an awareness of the other person's ability to absorb the information. The newer the relationship, the more this is so.

With friendship comes boundaries: understandings about what behavior is acceptable and what is not. When boundaries are tested, as they inevitably are, what can be forgiven and what cannot? Forgiveness may be considered an opening value in friendship and boundaries may be considered a closing value. The conversation between these values is what keeps human relationships going and growing. The vibrancy of this conversation is a measure of the individual's responsibility to the relationship as a whole.

Relationships that are mostly about "no" lead to negativity and are doomed to collapse. Branches of extended families sometimes battle against each other until they destroy the entire family. In the hope of restoring conversation, a marriage counselor may have to pry apart a husband and wife, locked as scorpions in a hateful embrace.

Social institutions flourish when they trust and honor their own versions of "yes" and "no." A long-term friendship or marriage can be a community. Families function best as communities. In community human beings work together toward a shared goal with a dynamic tension that converses between opening values, allowing freedom and creativity, and closing values that protect the group.

Organizations of all kinds depend upon their communal essence — the vibrancy of the conversation — to thrive and prevail against the inherent tendency of systems to disintegrate. Values in conversation allow human institutions to evolve, adapt and endure.

A chemical dependency rehabilitation center successfully treats thousands of seemingly hopeless cases by fostering an atmosphere of respect while maintaining rigorous behavioral standards that reflect the individual's responsibility to the community.

A liberal arts college thrives despite sky-rocketing costs and declining popular interest in the humanities. Faculty members are encouraged to be daring and innovative but also to uphold intellectual excellence. The acceptance of the typical excesses of adolescent students converses with firm academic and behavioral standards.

A military unit achieves effectiveness by combining top-down discipline with the officer corps' deference to the experience of the rank and file. The conversation between hierarchy and respect is the heartbeat of the service.

Business and professional firms survive beyond the lives of the founders because the quality of the enterprise is valued, along with the desire for profit. When the founder's ideals converse with the profit motive and the intense forces of competition, a private firm can plan for the long term, to benefit not only the owners but all the stakeholders: employees, customers, suppliers and the people who live in the town or city.

A vast wilderness preserved for human recreation and inspiration faces the conflict of pure preservation versus necessary intervention. Reverence for leaving nature undisturbed converses with the need for amenities to accommodate visitors. Other questions arise. Should forest fires be extinguished or allowed to take their destructive yet creative courses? Should dangerous animals be eliminated? Should overpopulated species be thinned?

Democracies are premised on the opening values of individual freedom acting in vibrant conversation with the closing values of the rule of law. Effective government results from a conversation between politicians and their constituents, balancing popular will with leadership. History shows the disastrous consequences of governing systems where the opening values of freedom, respect, dignity, diversity and creativity have been snuffed out by violence. Despotism, colonialism and racism are systems depending entirely upon restraining, categorizing, diminishing, imposing and denying — all closing values.

Effective philanthropy seeks a balance between the empowerment of economic assistance and the risk that charity will create dependency.

Science makes continuing advances because the spirit of discovery converses with the rigorous demands of the scientific method.

Meaningful lives are framed between living for the moment and planning for the future.

Society is a mass of relationships with complex strands of influence comprising a unity that has held together over time. We cannot master these infinite and ever-changing complexities, but we can understand the principles that apply to all systemic relationships. And we can identify trends in some of the most important elements of the systemic whole.

Another way of thinking about conversation between long and short-term values in human systems is to evaluate systems in terms of their thoughtfulness. Thoughtfulness includes the ability to consider mission, to examine honestly whether the mission is being accomplished and values upheld along the way, and to plan and implement course corrections to benefit the system for the long term. Distracted attention and fear lead to a focus on the short-term side of the conversational equation. Even in human endeavors whose underlying purpose is to preserve values — government, the learned professions, schools, charities and religion — the decline of thought fuels (and is fueled by) the tendency to capitalize the intangible. Principle then yields to exigency on account of the need, or perceived need, for money and the desire for power and prestige. The consequent decline of principle then becomes a way of life — a window frame through which people observe themselves and their surroundings. The decline of conversation in capitalism itself, the most pervasive and influential system in industrialized society, is a basic setting for this decline.

Public companies have gone multinational and shaped the burgeoning global economy. There is as much doubt about the power of the public company as about the power of nuclear weapons. But the economic success of the public company has come at a cost. Business is in moral decline largely because of a collapse in the conversation between opening and closing values in public corporations. This decline has substantial implications throughout society.

In capitalism, a mega-system, the owners have the right and obligation to define an enterprise's mission. The owners define both the opening values of the business — what it will do, what its standards will be, what it will mean in the world of commerce and the world at large — and the predominant closing value, which is the desired return on investment. The owners, in exchange for their investment, want the business to realize their vision while yielding a return on investment that is suitable, given the investment risk.

The owners of a hardware store in a small town understand their business and its role in the town economy as well as its profit potential. This sense of meaning also applies to a business operating in a national or international setting. Most enduring multinational companies exhibited flaws and shadow sides in their early years, but they stood for something greater than profitability. AT&T and Microsoft stood for innovation; CBS set high standards for broadcast journalism; the Morgan Bank stabilized the American financial system in the turbulent early years of the twentieth century.

In the contemporary world of public corporations, where shareholders concentrate more on stock price than the actual business, the conversation between the meaning of a business and its desire for profit is apt to collapse at the highest level of responsibility: ownership. This collapse reverberates throughout the system like a circle of falling dominoes. Managers are compensated for short-term results, employees are spurred on by positive and negative incentives to produce ever-increasing profits, quality yields to cost cutting. The result is that the firm's reputation, traditions and place in the community and world of commerce lack intrinsic significance and are attended to mainly for image enhancement and thus profit. The business becomes progressively more competitive, grueling, ruthless and inhumane, making misjudgment and collapse inevitable.

In contemporary civilization commerce dominates the landscape and the heart and mind. Our lives are immersed in work, consumption and commercial media. As commerce consumes time and attention, commercial values become more prominently branded upon the psyche. The collapse of conversation in the world of the public corporation sounds the moral tune for commerce and the way we live in general.

Caught in the cyclical interplay of fear and greed, the irresponsible personality attains predominance. The consequent breakdown in values pervades civilization, which increases fear and greed, which leads to thought and action that degrade values.

The declining conversation perpetuates itself and accelerates.

Complex mega-systems throughout civilization can be understood in terms of a collapse of conversation because of a default in the values, or long-term, side in favor of the short-term and pragmatic. Influential mega-systems such as law, politics, public education and religion can be understood as cycles in decline whose constituencies have lost track of their ideals. These powerful influences move through their own systemic infrastructures and flow inevitably into other social systems, into families and back into individual personalities.

It is possible — and necessary — to perceive all phenomena in which human beings are materially involved from the holistic perspective of systems: from international politics to neighborhood politics, from world religion to prayer groups, and from global climate change to community recycling practices. And a systems perspective enables us to appreciate the relationships among phenomena that seem unrelated. We might as easily say that it is possible and necessary to understand international politics in light of community recycling, and community recycling in light of world religion, and world religion in light of neighborhood politics, and neighborhood politics in light of global climate change, and global climate change in light of prayer groups.

The effects of conversational decline across mega-systems feed broadly into lesser social systems, into families and into individual personalities, and back again, without end, creating an infinitely dynamic and complex ecology of being.

Family

Family is like a tributary flowing in and out of the systemic swirl of existence. It influences the swirl and is influenced by it. It is important to understand how family works as a system, how an individual's role in a family shapes his way of knowing about the world, and how that way of knowing feeds into and leaves its own impression on all human systems.

A chamber orchestra playing a Bach concerto functions as a system. The notes define the roles of the individual instruments. The music proceeds through its polyphonic paces with two or three melody lines that make sense in relationship as each instrument calls and responds. The musicians play off one another. Should one musician come in a bit slow, the others in the ensemble adjust to maintain the tempo. The chamber orchestra is a patterned interaction of people playing together and of instruments sounding notes that weave together a meaningful whole.

A family works like a chamber orchestra, though less predictably because the score from which it plays contains less precise notation. Sometimes harmonious and often cacophonous, it would seem that there is no score at all. As a system, however, a family sends powerful messages to its members, sometimes assigning roles almost as precise as the orchestration of a Bach concerto, other times calling on the players to improvise. The quality and extent of the scoring in family systems shape not only the family group but the personalities of the individuals, who as adults become society.

The patterns of the family score are created in response to the survival instinct. As children we feel desperately in need of love from our parents, our protectors. Their dominance gives parents the means to score the family roles, and the individual needs of parents are highly influential in the decisions they make. Parents whose lives lack meaning may compose roles for their children that are intended to resolve the parents' own neediness. Children hang on Mother and Father's every word, inflection and gesture. They become adept at reading the signals and adapting their behaviors accordingly. The signals can be rigid and commanding. The roles become imprinted on young psyches.

How is this family music composed? Parents do not sit down at the kitchen table and write out the scores. Often collaboratively and almost always unconsciously, the identities of the parents, influenced strongly by their own experience as children, are the true composers. The resulting composition, scored to accommodate those identities, contains signals and rules that will shape the identities of the younger family players and the entire system.

Depending on how the parents experience themselves and each other, the notation will promote or constrain creativity and the fulfillment of individual potential.

Attempting to find security and meaning in their own lives through their children's lives, parents often induce in a child a strong will to achieve. Perhaps the child will go to a great university or accomplish impressive athletic feats. Having their child stand out from the crowd fulfills something missing in their sense of themselves. The heroic child is rewarded for accomplishment and neglected or derided for mediocrity or failure. Siblings, motivated by a desire to please their parents, cooperate in convincing the selected child to fulfill this role.

Every child wants the love of parents and siblings. If the family equates accomplishment with love, the child will accomplish. The child's self-concept and understanding of life depend on the intensity and consistency of this message, in which *Who I am* is equated with *What I accomplish. To fulfill my desire for love and safety, I must perform and be recognized for my achievements.*

Another common role — ironically, often in the same family — is played by the child who fails or gets in trouble repeatedly. Perhaps the repeated failures of one child highlight the successes of another. Perhaps the parents, feeling inadequate, find comfort in their superiority to the troubled one. Perhaps, if their marriage lacks intimacy, the parents compensate by fretting together over the troubled child. The family as a whole may derive its intimacy from its shared concern.

The child in this predicament may build his self-identity on difficulty. Have you ever been baffled by someone who shows great promise but who, at the last moment, falls short time and again?

Parents may train their children to mediate their marital conflicts. It may look like the go-between child is solving family problems, but it is more likely that the child is only providing a diversion. Family members resolve their controversies best by talking them out directly. If Mother and Father have conflicts, talking about their problems with their child instead of each other will perpetuate and probably increase the controversy. An intermediating child stands a good chance of becoming an adult who stands between relationships rather than being in them.

A parent in a troubled marriage may seek in a child what appears to be missing in the spouse. A child whose identity is tied in a spousal way to a parent is likely to experience betrayal and disappointment in the relationship. Such a child is likely to form assumptions on the basis of this experience that will shape future relationships.

The child also will respond to a score in which he is neglected because the parents are consumed with fulfilling their own needs. This child is likely to compensate for his unfulfilled needs by creating a persona that is designed to suit everyone except his authentic self. The person who dances to every tune but his own has wounds that do not heal easily and are likely to stand between that person and authenticity, or meaning, over a lifetime.

Children who grow up overly focused on the notes they are supposed to play for others have little sense of the music that comes from within. These children become adults who are committed not to their own individuality but to the roles assigned by their families. Often they find partners with complementary issues and the pattern is passed on to another generation.

One of the main characteristics of any system is its tendency to survive and keep exerting its qualitative influence. Systems may be disrupted or exposed to trauma, but they tend to restore and reassert themselves. These principles apply to families as well as to any human system.

Family members receive reinforcement for playing their roles and experience abandonment and threats of retribution for renouncing them. Rigid family systems exemplify the power of all human systems to hold people in behavior patterns that do not serve their real needs.

A daughter chosen to be the heroic one receives constant reinforcement for her achievement. But if she comes home with a low grade on her report card she will hear that her sour note has ruined the beautiful music. *What's the problem? You will never go to Harvard with those grades!*

A son is assigned the troublemaker role. The family orchestra may be playing a hand-wringing refrain, fretting about his repeated failures, imploring him to execute a virtuoso solo. What happens when the son shows signs of relinquishing the loser role assigned to him? *That won't work! You will screw it up just like everything else!*

A parent is trying to stop drinking. The family is forever berating the alcoholic parent, trying to convince him to stop. But after he's been on the wagon for a few days, someone mentions that he was more fun when he was drinking.

Individuals also protect their own roles in the family system. Let's say that I am the family joker, gaining attention by playing the buffoon. When I am alone I regret my self-belittling. I can be as serious as anyone and I wish people would accept me as I am. But when they encourage me to be the court jester and laugh at my jokes, I feel loved.

You are tired of being the star in the family. It's a burden, always striving to be the best, always tense about the possibility of falling short. But when your sibling receives recognition, you become jealous and feel that the recognition should be coming to you. You strive to get back into the limelight even though you are tired of it.

Systems tend to repair themselves. This explains why family members adopt the behavioral characteristics of recently deceased family members they did not resemble previously. The same phenomenon occurs in a family system where someone breaks free of an assigned role: another takes it on.

In a rigid family score, revisions are not welcomed. Subjects that threaten the prevailing order — like emotions, fears and deep yearnings — are not discussed. Discussions about death are rare. God, if mentioned at all, is invoked in support of the status quo. Active listening, which suggests curiosity and an appreciation for individual originality, is not practiced. Probing discussions about authority and the family's way of making decisions are taboo.

The child raised in a rigid family system takes its narrow viewpoint and constraining rules with him into society as an adult, imposing them on others and influencing the world according to them.

But it needn't be this way. Growing up can be an adventure, an ongoing discovery of *who I am*, what the world is and what is true beyond time and space. Experience peaks when self-consciousness disappears, and the question of *who I am* disappears with it. Self-realization depends on experience in the self-conscious phase of life. The chances of success are immensely greater when family has fertilized the soil of early growth with love.

As children mature they become aware of their own identities. Fulfillment of the basic mission of identifying oneself depends upon the interplay of subjective experience and objective reality. To learn about the world is to learn about oneself, and to learn about oneself is to learn about the world. The conversation between experience and the world is the topsoil in which meaning grows. The conversation depends upon the early emergence of the self, which in turn depends on how one is cared for as an infant and child.

Family nourishes and protects. In tandem with providing necessary nutrition, warmth, safety, healing and rest, the family provides affection. Family members open themselves to the infant by holding, rocking, kissing, singing and making funny noises to delight the infant. Fun, an extension of affection, feeds the spirit as nourishment feeds the body.

In family life the opening values bring out the child into his own consciousness. Good parents are watchers and listeners; they name what they observe. *I think you like fixing things. You are a fast runner.* As they watch and listen they affirm the importance of what the child sees as important. They affirm what the child feels, helping the child identify emotions for himself. *I see that you are sad. You seem happy this morning.* Support conveys the confidence of the parent and assures the child that he is capable of attaining his own aspirations. *You want to learn to ride a bicycle, and you can. You can achieve your academic goals.* These early practices help create self-awareness and a sense of the self's significance. *I am important. I am loved. I have dreams. I am good at this and not so good at that. I want. I can.*

Opening values include respect, which means listening to the child's feelings and opinions and valuing them as reflections of the person and in the listening process, validating the self.

Trust gives the freedom to fulfill, or not, a responsibility. Trust is a grant of opportunity. The child sensibly trusted is given the experience of autonomy. Trust enables children to see themselves as beings with free will: *I have the car; I can find alcohol to drink though I am not supposed to. What choice shall I make?*

Opening values include forgiveness, which is often mistakenly interpreted as forgetting the wound inflicted by another. What occurs when we try to forget a serious hurt is not forgetting but a repression of emotions that spring up later, unexpectedly and counterproductively. Forgiveness applies where the pain is remembered and felt. *You have hurt me; now what?* Forgiveness means not ending the relationship even though there has been unforgotten pain.

Opening values in the family must be tempered by the closing value of boundaries. Parents struggle with boundaries, a concept simple in description and difficult in application. Boundaries define the limitations on acceptable behavior, making clear what parents expect of their children and what the consequences will be when these expectations are not met. *If you throw your cereal onto the floor there will be no more food until the next meal. If you want a bicycle you must earn money for it.*

Meaningless carping at children is not setting boundaries. Describing boundaries and then abandoning them is not setting boundaries. Articulating rules without consequences is not setting boundaries. The failure to set boundaries creates a personality that is like a body without bones and skin.

Children resist boundaries, yet they unconsciously seek them for self-definition. Boundaries and guidance are necessary to make one's way in the world, to achieve competence and to do so consistently with one's values.

Children adopt the values of their parents. Parents who are truthful, generous and disciplined are likely to raise children with these qualities. By modeling these important closing values, parents earn the moral authority to insist upon them. Parents also display opening values such as forgiveness and flexibility. The vibrancy and consistency of the parental conversation between opening and closing values is virtually certain to be carried into the next generation.

Religious practice in family contains its own conversation. Religion is an opening value in that it confirms meaning in life despite the ambiguity inherent in struggling to live while death is certain. Religion is a closing value in that the existence of truth, which is the premise of religion, means that something is required of human beings.

The opening values of parental and familial love contain elements of letting go. The culminating and perhaps most difficult part of being a parent is allowing children, when they become young adults, to pursue their own dreams and live their own lives. The older parent may be there for the adult child, but the basic responsibility must now be given over. By caring for their children at all stages of development and recognizing them finally as autonomous adults, loving parents do themselves voluntarily out of a job whose compensations are enormous.

Every family is different. Every family is entitled to its own vision. Every family has distinct rituals and traditions. And no family attains perfection, which is not a concept relevant to process in general — certainly not to family. Process exists because of imperfection, love's ally. The imperfection of families and family members sets the stage for process and makes the opening and closing values of love meaningful and necessary.

In the vibrant family as chamber ensemble, the composition is designed both to accommodate the needs of the group and to encourage making music that is uniquely that of the individual players. When family members are able to play harmoniously together, but still according to their unique individuality, they feed love back into the family system and out into all the systems that comprise existence.

Self

The self is also a system, a revolving process in which human beings experience and generate spirit, the fuel of ascending, enduring human systems. The vibrant self is the first spiral — the spiral at the center. The potential reach of its spirit is the entire realm of existence.

Experience

Experience is an active, influential process that bestows significance.

The hardest and best work I do is listening. When I listen intently I begin to know the person speaking to me. My knowledge goes beyond facts. I respond emotionally and intuitively. The other in turn experiences my empathy, which releases and opens him. His opening opens me. Our shared experience is continuous and mutually creative. I experience the one I listen to deeply and in the process of my experience I become him, and he becomes me.

Experience can be mundane or exquisite, but its potential is unbounded by space or time.

A painting of a snow-covered haystack reminds you of winter years ago and you feel again what it is like to be young in a cold place.

The remembrance of an ancient loss comes upon you suddenly and you have to struggle for breath as you did when the loss hit you the first time.

There is a moment when all the lover desires is to know the beloved, a yearning more profound and comprehensive than sexual desire. In such a moment the beloved is transformed from body into essence, becoming not a person with pleasing characteristics such as strength, beauty or wisdom but strength, beauty or wisdom themselves. The experience transforms the lover as well. Fear dissipates and the lover desires not to possess but to release.

Experience takes more than mere awareness. What you can see you may not observe; what stirs your auditory nerves you may not hear; you can be unaware of your own emotions. You are not looking; you are not listening; perhaps you are too busy for feelings, or trauma has separated you from them. Whatever the reason, the physics of awareness is present but *you* are not. If *you* are present in body but absent in spirit, there can be no experience.

Experience means being present and it means owning awareness. It means *I* am aware. Something is happening to *me* and, for a split second or for a lifetime, *I* notice it. To some extent, great or small, *I* care about it.

Self

In order for there to be experience there must be an *I* and a *me* — in other words, a self.

At birth and in early infancy there is no *I* and therefore no self. In the baby's dim perception the caregivers — the enormous and all-powerful — are universal. The baby has instinctive urges but no sense that these urges belong to anyone. There is an urge to eat but *I am hungry* does not apply. What happens does not happen to *me*, it just happens.

Earliest experience, circumscribed by instinct and fear, takes on the human characteristics of *I* and *me* when an awareness of agency emerges from the fog of infant consciousness. There is, at first, a faint perception of cause and effect. The infant gets a hint: not only did the cereal dish fly off the high chair and crash on the floor, but *I* was involved. *My body did something that I wanted!* This revelation establishes the identity of a separate being with an independent will and ability to act — in other words, *me.*

Let's try that again! (Has a baby ever once thrown food to the floor and not tried it again?)

The discovery of *me* begins the self-awareness and self-creating that is the self.

I have a self when I realize that *I* am *me.* The self is made in *I's* perception of *me* and the integration of this perception into who I understand *myself* to be. *I made the dish crash on the floor! I made the big people pick it up!* Delightful revelations such as these establish a separate identity and begin the ongoing process of the self.

Parental affirmation — helping a child identify his talents, personality traits, aspirations and emotions — provides a crucial boost to forming a self. Parental boundaries — such as discouraging flying dishes — give context to the self the way skin gives context to the body.

When *I* am aware of *me* and when this awareness leads to knowledge and an acceptance of *me* and an incorporation of *me* into *who I am* — I have a self.

The self is a dynamic, evolving self-awareness. The self is comparable to painting a portrait of oneself painting a self-portrait.

The infant has the task of establishing a self separate from the caregivers. As the infant grows the task becomes broader in scope — more aspects of identity emerge such as skills, ideas and nuanced emotions; more people with whom to identify and from whom to separate; and the beginning of responsibility.

The dramatic story of a human life is of self interacting with the world and, simultaneously, self interacting with the self. Literature, art and music may be interpreted in light of this dynamic tension.

Every flicker of human experience contains an element of self-knowing because experience depends upon the self and, by involving the self, helps form the self. You may see and hear well, but without a vibrant self, experience is dim. When the self is burning bright what you learn teaches you about yourself because of the self-awareness that is present in the other-awareness.

The vibrant self is naturally curious. Curiosity leads to learning, which yields world awareness and self-awareness, world understanding and self-understanding, world esteem and self-esteem, and compassion for oneself, for others and for life itself.

Spirit

Spirit is the energy — the real but intangible essence — of the *I/me* relationship. The self is a conductor of love. The energy of the self manifests this love: eternal and universal and at the same time immanent in the human spirit. Something so here-and-now as self-awareness is, literally, divine.

The spirit's potential can be seen in our unique capacity as human beings to decide to override instinctive fear or desire and to act upon belief. As the spirit grows, our human capacity to learn and change grows with it.

When the capacity and will to change are present and change occurs, the spirit expands and exerts a corresponding influence on its surroundings.

Spirit heals systems, conjoins them peacefully and moves them to ascend as spirals. Spirit imbues existence with its quality through experience. Thus the vibrant self can listen creatively. The vibrant self can be inspired by beauty, feel universal agony and universal joy and love so completely as to free the beloved. The vibrant self can transcend time and space. It can create existence by giving meaning.

The spirit is not invincible. Its vitality depends on the condition of the self. Trauma or neglect may diminish the spirit and even extinguish it. But the energy of the vibrant self — love issuing from an evolving *I/me* relationship — expands, aspiring to realize its universal potential.

The spirit is ignited and strengthened in the lifelong process of realizing the self. Becoming who you are is a transmigration — from self-ignorance to self-awareness, world ignorance to world awareness, separation to unity, the finite to the universal— in short, from fear to love.

Existence

The world has height and width and weight and density. The world is physics, a collection of ephemera. A turn takes place when you come to the self, from manifestation to essence — from existing to existence itself.

A human being is, to begin with, a physical reality. Spirit is an intangible phenomenon arising from tangible flesh. The crucial turn that takes place in the self is that of the physical melding into the spiritual.

Spirit, the predicate of the uniquely human phenomenon of experience, gives meaning both to the subject having the experience and to the object experienced. The human spirit endows the world with meaning and therefore existence.

This is not to say that there is no physical matter without human experience. But without experience there is no significance: matter doesn't matter. The human spirit is the *being* part of the human being and the *being* part of the physical world.

The human spirit is existence itself. The quality of existence is the vitality of the spirit.

The spirit empowers the human being to engage in conversation between instinctive desire and principle, listening to principle and choosing to follow it. The spirit inspires the individual to see beyond the apparent complexity of the world. The spirit enables the individual to experience unity.

Movement across the arc of life and the expansion of the spirit fuel each other. Virtues like courage and compassion simultaneously endow and are nourished by the spirit.

The dramatic action takes place necessarily on the stage of the world, but the drama is the self.

Like the blades of a ceiling fan, the revolutions of perception and assumption that are the self begin slowly and gain speed. Early on each blade captures the attention of the observer. As the blades gain momentum and move faster they become a blur. At high speed only a vague film remains, through which one can easily see. Self-consciousness yields to consciousness of unity with only the slightest film of an ego-self remaining.

At the ending of life it is not only possible but acceptable and even desirable to pass through the film.

Part II
The Arc of Life

The Ground of the Self

Spirit and spiral go together. The spirit can elevate human systems and cause them to become ascending spirals. The spirit can reverse declining systems and move them toward ascension. But decline has the advantage of momentum and weakens the spirit.

Fear and desire move humanity away from the spirit. The suffering that accompanies fear and desire seeks remedies and immediate solutions from the world. Humanity suffers and tilts instinctively toward the world. Meaning declines and the spirit declines. As a result the world gets worse and as it does, the tilt toward the world becomes more pronounced, and the spirit declines further. And the world gets worse.

The spirit retains its potential to assuage fear and desire with love and to raise humanity above itself. But think of the challenge. Humanity is placed in the impermanent world and challenged to find eternal truth. With all the demands that survival places upon us, it would seem that we are set up to fail. How can we satisfy our bodily needs and protect our lives and at the same time evolve beyond our bodies and even our lives themselves?

The essential human challenge is the constant need for reinvigoration of the spirit in a world that puts the spirit down. The only response equal to this challenge is a determination to realize the self. This determination requires courage that must sometimes be blind. The energy for this demanding leap of faith is found upon the ground of the self.

The pathway to meaning is the pathway to saving the world. It is also found upon the ground of the self.

What happens without the spirit is just the world — particles without significance. Without the spirit the human being is without significance. The spirit can raise the human part of the world above the world — above ourselves. It can shape destiny. The spirit rises from the ground of the self.

Crucial transitions — from body to spirit, world to universal, craving to meaning, instinct to principle — describe crossing the arc of life, from fear to love. Living requires action in the world, but crossing the arc of life takes place in the world that is apart from the world — the ground of the self.

Fear and Closing

Movement across the arc of life refers to realization of the self: the fulfillment of the highest potential and duty of the human being. The ground on which this passage to significance takes place is that of the self. The span of the self is from fear to love. Here a new perspective is gained and the world becomes important mainly in the service of living a significant life.

Crossing the arc of life may sound small in scope: it takes place not on the ground of empires but of the self. When you get to know the self, however, you realize its grandeur.

Love flows from the vibrant self, contributing creative energy, compassion, healing and beauty to the systems of existence, which feed back to the self. When a person is frightened his fear pervades the systems of existence and contributes fear to the ecology of being. This fear feeds back to the self.

Experience is not simply the passive observation of information; it is participation of the most fundamental kind. Therefore, how we know — the assumptions that frame our experience — contributes to the quality of humankind's influence in the world.

As we attempt to cross the arc of life from fear to love, our passage through the wilderness is constrained by assumptions, or frames, which, like window frames, highlight and limit. Culture creates frames by feeding values back to the self. Frames are implicit in messages delivered by business, politics, government, education, charity, entertainment and religion. We adopt these frames as the infrastructure of the prevailing wisdom. Families contribute to constraints through values passed on in family systems. We adopt the frames of family life because we adapt to them in the most formative time of our lives.

Individual experience contributes. The fearful individual, harnessed by narrow frames and unable to learn, interprets the world narrowly. His frames are apt to narrow as he goes. The more secure person learns through interaction with the world. To learn is to open the windows and expand the frames.

Frames become engraved in the mind. They shape our perceptions and shape the stories we tell ourselves and our associates, friends, lovers and children. They become manifest in the stories told to the world by our lives.

The animal in fear, including the human animal, cares about results. I am running for my life pursued by a hungry tiger. Do I care about the vegetation I am trampling? Do I appreciate the beauty of the green jungle trees against the pure blue sky? Does it matter that I am trespassing on someone's property? Am I concerned with the needs of the tiger? The life-preserving instinct floods my being and fixes my concentration on a single project: saving my skin! In the purely pragmatic frame there is no ambiguity, no opposition to resolve, no confusing paradox, no irony, no humor and no acceptance. The pragmatic frame excludes nuance and subtlety. Process is nothing. My cries to God are about my hide, not my soul.

We are never more like beasts than when we are in fear. If there is meaning in escaping the hungry tiger, it equates squarely to survival. Survival is essential, but as a one-dimensional, pragmatic experience it does not involve the multidimensional, textured self. There is no room for self-awareness in the purely result-oriented frame and no sense of functioning within a greater whole.

Fear, not circumstance, is the fundamental issue. When I am afraid of the tiger behind me, my life actually may be at risk or it may not. The tiger may be a kitten enlarged in my imagination. The tiger may be chasing me for a playful romp in the meadow. The tiger may be a creation of my imagination entirely. The influence of fear — whether realistic or irrational, specific or generalized — excludes qualitative things and narrows frames.

Our intelligence and our ability to achieve desired results have preserved the human species and caused it to flourish and dominate the world. Because of our practical skills and our determination, we have the wherewithal to turn the abundant resources of the world to our advantage and survive as individuals, families and societies. Results orientation and the creative energy that fear and desire contribute have accomplished much that is good.

Now, having built the infrastructure of survival, post-survival humanity has a different need: to find meaning. The anachronistic persistence of the survival mentality in post-survival circumstance has demoralized humankind and perverted our abundance, sending us back toward primitive chaos.

Fear, which has served us well, has overrun humanity and threatens its existence.

We are born in fear and hammered from early childhood into pragmatic beings who perceive significance predominantly in ends. We learn to place our faith in what we have, what others think of us and what we accomplish. We value what we do and how we appear over who we are. We go about life as if meaning were outside us. We focus on results and neglect process.

In the result-oriented mindset we perceive reality according to what is useful. Our vision narrows as we focus on what we need in order to get the results we want. The more pragmatic we are, the narrower the concern for quality. Focusing on ends and neglecting the quality of our means, we blow upon the hot coals of fear and desire, send the self into a downward spiral and create an ever-lurking tiger from which we cannot escape.

Every human being has problems to solve. We must eat, be warm and protect ourselves from illness and injury. So we must be, to some extent, results-oriented. But in a world of abundance there is scant discrimination between what we need to sustain life and what we desire, attempting to satisfy our quest for meaning.

Over time we adopt belief systems that accommodate our results orientation. We justify our actions in stories we tell about the world. Slavery, colonization and discrimination are justified by stories about racial superiority. Messianic movements spin stories that play on human despair and justify despotism, war-mongering and genocide. The excesses of capitalism, which yield concentrated wealth amid widespread poverty, are undergirded by social Darwinism's concept of prosperity of the fittest. Plundering the environment is justified by deifying the marketplace. Religion is twisted to support hierarchy and violence. Nationalistic myths justify international aggression. Blame and dependency support a culture of irresponsibility. These stories are passed on from generation to generation.

Primitive humankind came to grips with thunder and lightning by understanding them as expressions of the gods. Lacking information about the world, our ancestors filled in the gaps with imagination and belief. Understanding required faith and culture supported faith: to go against faith was to depart from the prevailing ethos. Science is filling in the information gaps. The explosion of useful information from science and technology over the past four centuries challenges the preeminence of faith, creating skepticism in our culture about the validity of belief without demonstrable proof. Today the way of faith is a departure from the prevailing ethos.

The scientific method of analysis breaks the whole into parts, regards parts independently of wholes, thinks in terms of causes with linear effects and doubts what cannot be observed and measured. Science has elevated reason over intuition, thought over emotion and manifestation over mystery.

Science has brought a multitude of beneficial changes to human existence; these need hardly be catalogued here. It is sufficient to say that for most of the industrialized and technologized world, the practical problems that defined life in the Middle Ages have been eradicated. Opportunities to enjoy and create have been opened at heights unimagined by the most fertile medieval minds. In the world made possible by science there has been a recognition of human dignity: the establishment of individual rights has reduced oppression.

The great discoveries and developments of the last two centuries have come mainly from scientists, as have the roots of the most awful devastations. It is no wonder that in the extreme of scientific experience we feel able to play God.

The shadow side of the scientific mindset is that it has crowded out the intuitive, holistic ways of knowing that preceded it, feeding the human tendency to focus on results. We seek to deal with existence as if we were scientifically detached from it rather than part of an indivisible unity. The foreign policy of powerful nations is premised on aggrandizement and violence, which fly directly against unity. Playing God is an understandable but perilous enterprise.

Unbalanced, the scientific mindset closes too tightly the curtains of perception. As we see the world only in parts, consisting of scarce resources for which we must compete — a lonely, hostile environment — we act in ways that make it so.

Fear and science then feed each other in a symbiotic relationship that is itself a system in geometric decline. The fearful mind fulfills its prophecy.

Western culture emphasizes the belief that human beings are separate and independent by nature and right. This doctrine, known as atomism, emerged from the eighteenth-century European Enlightenment. The Enlightenment moved civilization away from slavish religiosity and held up human beings as independent individuals deserving respect and possessing inherent rights. Relationship to other people and to the living world declined in importance as the atom, which refers to the individual human being, came to the fore. Antagonism replaced interdependence. Rational, scientific thinking, with its tendency to break down into parts, became a way of knowing.

The United States was founded by people of the Enlightenment; the American way of knowing to this day celebrates individual accomplishment, individual prosperity and individual rights. Our leading thinkers are, like Jefferson and Madison, rational, respectful but skeptical of religion, adherents to law and problem solvers.

Scarcity as a frame flows from atomism. We apply the classical physics of time and space to our conception of reality. We see resources as limited and people as autonomous and we conclude that the competitive marketplace is the ideal mechanism for allocating scarce resources. Business, government, education and even charity and religion operate on principles of supply and demand restrained by law and the invisible hand of the market. Social Darwinism — the idea that the strong survive the competitive test and the weak fall to the side — is the underlying ethos.

Whereas the Age of Faith emphasized belief and the human heart, the Age of Science focused on reason and action. Today we believe that the emotions that motivate do not cause: only a person's actions yield discernible effects. We believe that the moral quality of how we experience the world has no immediate influence on the condition of the world. In this frame rational thought is considered more reliable than intuition and emotion has no intrinsic relevance. Action plans and useful information are more valuable than attention to process. What is done is more important than how. Experience is something people receive and does not directly influence the nature of things or the experience of others.

We believe in assessment, in applying our knowledge to the evaluation of a person, place or thing in authoritative, qualitative terms. We feel we may adjudge someone good or evil. We derive comfort in doing so, placing ourselves apart from and above someone or something else. In moral judgments certainty is prized over ambiguity. What is called justice, but is really retribution, is prized over forgiveness. Blame dominates the public discourse. Colonialism, nationalism and racism are made morally possible by assessment; violence, both subtle and obvious, is justified by it. In daily life we gossip, slight others and pass judgment.

The problem with frames is what we miss. We see in parts rather than wholes, in separation rather than unity. Frames for thought and action often bring short-term success. In our efforts to solve the problems of fear by focusing on and managing external conditions, we engrave frames in our thinking, and our thought and action move others to adopt them. As belief systems they seem to require no validation. We do not examine the quality of means we deem necessary to accomplish the ends we deem crucial.

As success leads to success we become more dependent upon the underlying principle and it becomes firmly fixed in the mind. Even if we have failed to find overall contentment, there are many pleasures and other diversions. We cling to the moral premises as we would grasp the handrails on a ship in a storm.

Seeing the world for all purposes through frames created by science is a tilt toward the material world, away from the spirit, which casts a shadow and creates more fear.

When people compete for scarce vital resources violence is inevitable. The ethos of violence is irresponsibility, the sense that the consequences of what one does are not within the moral realm of the actor. Although competition can be productive, it runs amok and becomes destructive when unchecked by responsibility.

Violence pervades social intercourse in obvious ways; we are so used to them we don't see them as violent. Cruelty is a cause but lives on as an effect. Greed owns the owner and inspires greed in others. Striking enervates the one who strikes as well as the victim; killing deadens the spirit of the killer. We are afflicted by a scientific myopia, conceptualizing violence as occurring over space and time in a single cause and effect direction. This is thinking in straight lines and parts: the conception of violence as a one-way force polluting parts without polluting the whole.

In this frame we employ well-intended violence as an instrument to solve the problem of malevolent violence, carrying on the myth of violent heroics that is central to Western culture from Greek gods to Crusaders to cowboys. We premise our foreign policy on violence, believing that the ability to effect catastrophic violence elsewhere will make us safe. It would be unwise to say that foreign policy should never involve violence or to try to draw a line defining good and bad violence. But any decision about violence must emerge from a deep awareness that violence harms in all directions.

We create the world by how we conceive it. The world responds by manifesting and reinforcing the mindset that created it.

In the rationalistic mindset we deny the simultaneous presence of opposing qualities. We believe in heroes driving out villains and in living happily ever after. We see in joy an absence of sadness and in loss an absence of gain. We see masculinity and femininity as mutually exclusive. Some see natural beauty naively as harmless and innocent; others see natural resources as elements to be exploited in a hostile environment. We believe that the shadow can be forced out of the light by right action. We see death as an opponent to life and we live our lives as contests against death.

Our inability or unwillingness to appreciate the ambiguity inherent in living causes us to stumble, and our narrow-mindedness prevents us from learning from our mistakes. Instead of expanding our horizons we interpret occurrences in light of our misconceptions and denigrate those who do not share our point of view.

We deny the shadow in ourselves and justify our abuse and neglect of others by blaming their darkness. One religion despises another; one race, one political party, one nation, one family, one individual. The stories we tell in fear blame others, place ourselves on the moral high ground and provide the justification for irresponsibility.

From the tilt toward the world and away from the spirit has come wonderful abundance and depressing materialism, individual freedom imperiled by individualistic irresponsibility, decency corrupted by self-righteousness and moral superiority, the confusion of justice and revenge, the decline of authenticity and the misconception that fear can be eradicated by the use of violence.

Will to the Self

When the survival instinct is satisfied we instinctively want to know who we are. The drive to answer the question *Who am I?* stands just behind the will to survive. We seek food, we seek warmth, we seek to mate, we seek ourselves.

Life responds, presenting human beings with ordeals that raise the specter of mortality so that we have the opportunity to struggle; in struggling we find ourselves and in finding ourselves we move from fear to love. This is the truth expressed in heroic legend and literature. The hero must confront monsters and bizarre conundrums from which there is no evident escape. The hero seems small and vulnerable. The hero must be brave and intelligent, must endure body blows, must believe in himself and experience his own frailty, to fulfill his destiny — to rise above.

In the epic medieval poem, "Sir Gawain and the Green Knight," a fearsome Green Knight appears in the court of King Arthur and proposes a remarkable game. "Take my sword and deal me your mightiest blow. But a year from now you must find me at the green chapel and submit to such a blow from me." Young Gawain, a virtuous knight, accepts the challenge and promptly decapitates the Green Knight.

But the Green Knight does not die. He picks up his head, mounts his horse and rides away. Gawain must find the green chapel and receive a blow in return from the Green Knight.

Alone, Gawain rides through the unknown forest, facing hardship and hostility, in order to fulfill his promise to the Green Knight. Can you imagine a young man riding alone through the forest to certain doom? Why would he make the trip at all? Why not just slip away and avoid the confrontation?

Along the way Gawain seeks shelter and is welcomed into the castle of a nobleman and his beautiful wife. Gawain agrees to give his host whatever he receives while a guest at the castle. After three unsuccessful attempts to seduce Gawain, the nobleman's wife gives Gawain her girdle, a magic garment that will protect him from death. Gawain conceals the gift from the nobleman.

Gawain arrives at last for his appointment with the Green Knight, prepared to receive the return blow. The Green Knight raises his ax as if to decapitate Gawain. Instead he nicks Gawain slightly on the neck, saying, "This wound is for your deception in keeping the girdle." Established by ordeal as a hero and wounded slightly as evidence of his human frailty, Gawain emerges as a complete Arthurian knight.

The hero responds to struggle and loss without abandoning principle. He is honest, brave, loyal, humble and charitable; but he is human. He need not be perfect, but he must endeavor to rise above human weakness. The hero's character is best described as responsible. The hero is not unafraid; the hero overcomes fear by facing it, and the reward is the self.

The will to the self, demonstrated by the lonely journey to an uncertain fate, is no anachronism even in an age often described as post-heroic. The abundance of our day offers the opportunity and intensifies the need to find meaning. But we have no authentic heroic archetype, and it is tempting to pursue diversions or stay at home instead of making the hero's journey to the self with its many hardships and dangers. Young Gawain riding alone through the wilderness to face the Green Knight is an image to keep in mind.

Although we lack the wisdom and moral strength to make the heroic journey, the will to the self is no less compelling than it was in Arthurian times. The difference between the heroic archetype and the contemporary reality lies in how we respond to our will to find ourselves.

Teenagers desperately seek autonomy from those who have towered over them — the adults who have served as their *de facto* selves. Their self-concepts are still heavily dependent on the affirmation of others because the mechanism for internal recognition is not wholly developed yet. This generates the push-me/pull-me syndrome of the adolescent years. To attend to the teenager is to perpetuate the oppression; not attending leaves the teenager feeling neglected. Some seek approval, defiance is common. Behind both are unspoken questions: *What do you think of me? Who am I?*

The will to the self does not end upon completion of the adolescent years. The messages of the post-survival world offer seductive responses to the hero's question *Who am I?* Advertising is dedicated to affirming the identity of the target audience and tying that affirmation to a product. Mass media respond to the same aching demand. Entertainment confirms our fears and prejudices, lends us an identity and relieves our feelings of impotence. The absurd dynamic of popular culture shows how we hunger for selves and how short we have fallen in attempting to find them.

We want to go where the hero goes, but we are reluctant to take the hero's risk and, even if we have the courage, we lack information about where the journey takes place and how to make it authentically. The individual and collective self rest upon an increasingly inauthentic and insubstantial foundation.

This is the cyclical conundrum of the self and the world. As we find ourselves less and less, we are willing less and less to take the risk actually required to find ourselves. So the will to the self remains unsatisfied, leaving us as confused as in adolescence.

As we lose the capacity to develop ourselves, we are caught in a spiral in which love is depleted and fear gains momentum. The fearful selves that generate fearful selves are projected onto the screen of the world. The world is then played back as videotape in the minds of the seekers, falsely stimulating or assuaging, leading to lives of escalating fear, endlessly spiraling.

The ecology of being includes the environment, war and peace, poverty and plenty, culture, family and the quest for meaning. The self is at the center of this ecology. In the poor and war-torn regions human beings face a chronic struggle for survival. In the wealthy, stable regions the struggle is to move through the wilderness of self-consciousness to the authenticity of the self.

Meaning

We are born in fear. The infant is a bawling mass of instinct, a cub with a mission to survive, preoccupied and frantically pragmatic. Process means nothing. Ends are all. Contentment is possible only when every want is satisfied.

Many people do not progress much beyond this stage. In fear human beings revert to the primeval condition, thinking and acting in survival mode regardless of whether survival is actually at stake. Fear may be with us in times of real threat and at other times as the psychological residue of infancy, when we were very much in need of loving safekeeping. With the benefit of love we can emerge from the defensive survival mode into the expansive mode of learning and caring. When we overcome, even temporarily, our aboriginal obsession with not-dying, we are making our way across the arc of life.

But life contains an overarching irony. We know that ultimately we will not survive. The quest for life will be lost. Death waits, lurking in the unconscious mind, flushed into consciousness by changes that connote endings. We know this — alone among all animals — but amazingly our knowledge does not defeat us. We work at life even though we know that life ends. Some people fall by the wayside in depression or self-destructiveness. But most keep going with a persistence that suggests a belief that meaning can be found in the human experience and that meaning trumps death.

There are other answers to the problem of death awareness. One is that death is not death but birth into eternal life. Life after death is an important concept in organized religion, relieving fear and motivating proper conduct by promising the rewards of heaven or the punishments of hell. The belief in life after death offers comfort and meaning. The fear of death may be overcome not only by belief in eternal life but by overcoming fear itself. It is possible to resolve the problem of death by living a meaningful life.

Fear moves the mind away from now to then. It doesn't matter how lovely the view is when escaping the pursuing tiger. Panic may be quite valid and my efforts to remedy the situation quite important, but without process — an awareness of now — there is no meaning. I will not remember happily my time escaping the tiger. The foot race means nothing, only the anticipated result.

So many things in life are like that: single-mindedly pursuing money, manipulating, hurrying, arguing, blaming, avoiding, fighting, accusing, acquiring — these may bring results but not lasting satisfaction.

The motivating emotions behind meaninglessness — greed, envy, jealousy, anger and desire — are the sibling children of fear. Honesty, courage, integrity, charity, commitment and care are the offspring of love. Love concerns now. Love offers meaning. I refer to love in its endless variety, in every aspect of life in which the spirit flows out from the individual and engages the world.

Fear and love speak to each other over the common ground of the self. Human beings are meant to move across this ground from fear to love. We do so in small steps through the wilderness, which is the setting of the heroic journey, with missteps and back steps. In that progression is meaning.

Failure in the wilderness passage — meaninglessness — is the epidemic humankind endures in a fragmented, declining existence. It is the evidence of the cyclical struggles that imperil humanity.

We wonder today whether authentic heroism is possible. But heroism exists all around us. Men and women struggle to learn a trade, a craft, a profession. We create families and raise children. We have great teachers who refuse to give up on learning. Farmers do battle with the unpredictable elements. People volunteer and give money to charity.

Heroism — responsible behavior — remains possible despite the disjointedness of the age. The question is whether we are able to make the decision to act heroically.

Life puts us through hell as it frustrates our aspirations and takes away our comfort. Sometimes we are meant to overcome these blockades and deprivations, mustering strength and persevering in the journey toward what we seek. Sometimes we are meant simply to endure. Throughout life there are losses and endings to be suffered: losses of health and comfort, trust, relationship; losses of knowing and of the hope to know; losses of youth and losses of life. Even change for the better means loss. Every change in the constantly changing narrative of life is in some way an ordeal.

How will we overcome or endure ordeal? Our suffering does not entitle us to anything. This is the most difficult lesson to learn. We are asked not only to suffer but to suffer in the right way. By enduring an ordeal without abandoning our citizenship in the unity, we accomplish the hero's mission of finding ourselves. I neither seek suffering nor wish it upon anyone; yet I know that going through an ordeal without abandoning principle is the road to the self.

Suffering is by no means the only way to meaning. Meaning can be found in work. Some people are endowed with special abilities; they find their niche, learn as apprentices and then practice as professionals. As they explore and perfect their talents, they add their special mark. In work one may find meaning by aspiring to the ideal of the process itself. Work is not always fascinating; sometimes one can only try to find meaning in it by doing an uninteresting job in the right way.

Meaning is found in relationship, which involves the delightful experience of coming together and the necessary ordeal of loss. We create relationships in instants and throughout lifetimes. As we learn more about the other we learn about ourselves. We struggle through the adjustments that must be made in order to accommodate.

We endure our disappointments and feel remorse over the suffering we inflict. We struggle to forgive, preserving the meaning in relationship and perhaps enhancing it. We suffer in the loss of relationship by death or departure.

There is meaning in the experience of beauty. Some things are beautiful to almost everyone, but the ability to experience beauty in its most exquisite repositories requires aesthetic training and concentration. There is meaning in taking on a discipline such as flower arranging or painting, in which one seeks to understand and create beauty. One can measure the decline of meaning in places of extreme poverty by the disappearance of beauty. At the other extreme, but for similar reasons, opulence can be lustrous but lack beauty.

Most of us have places where we are at peace, or where we fell in love, or where we learned to learn. We treasure these places in memory and we experience them as if we were there, then. I recall fall days, dry and anticipatory, at my college; winter nights as a child with snow falling past the street lamp in front of our house; green spring days of baseball with my sons; the summer morning smell of pine on the ranch where I worked as a teenager — and the experience returns.

Meaning is found in the feeling of being beyond space and time, the realization that one spirit is within all and all are within one. I experience this sometimes while listening to beautiful music; I can see it in the face of the musician performing the piece as well. I experience it in moments of what Jung called synchronicity, as when someone mentions an obscure, out-of-print book and it finds me the next day in a used book shop, or when I hear a new word and then hear it again three times in the same week, or when someone I love thinks of something in the precise moment I do. I experience it hiking in the country when my mind lets go of where I started, where I'm going and how long it will take to get there. Time then means nothing; I am flooded with the presence of people and places long gone, not as recollections but now, and I accept this reality as I do in dreams. In moments of joy I feel the joy of the world; in moments of suffering I feel its suffering.

Moments such as these are religious experience. The practice of opening and extending to the ideal makes the mundane meaningful. This is life lived as prayer. Not every moment is about creative or expressive work, loving relationship, moving beauty or place, or miraculous synchronicity. Most of life is not quality time, high or low. Beyond survival and between suffering and peak experience, belief illuminates the mundane and motivates the traveler to endure with integrity and authenticity.

Lack of meaning and lack of self are the same. When meaning is not within I must have it from without. Small things upset me when I have no compelling sense of context, of what I am about. Someone criticizes me. I don't get the seat I wanted on the airplane. Someone fails to give me the credit I feel I deserve. The failure of the world to affirm me is devastating, triggering fear and causing me to react angrily or desperately. If I have purpose these things are mere annoyances; I move on.

What we seek is experience that has intrinsic value, here and now, in this life. In the long run it doesn't matter what others think of us or what we have or who loves us and who does not. People, places and things do not satisfy human beings in the long run. The predicate for satisfaction in experience is the relationship of *I* and *me*. I have enough when I am enough.

I have done enough when I am enough. I am recognized and regarded enough when I am enough. I exert enough power when I am enough. I am loved enough when I am enough.

When experience and meaning are present I contribute positively to the cycles comprising the unity of existence. My actions are conjunctive, uniting *I* and *me*, uniting my self with all living things and in doing so, exerting the elevating influence of love from the center of the ecology of being.

Choice

The signal distinction of human nature is our capacity to change for purely moral reasons. We can take responsibility for shaping the world according to our perception of truth. We can rise above ourselves.

The material world is energy. All phenomena arise from this energy: matter and force organized in systems that produce life and consciousness. Classical physics led the scientifically inclined to suspect that all of existence, including human thought and action, was simply a swirl of particles in motion acting and interacting according to universal rules. Human beings may imagine that they can make choices, free-will skeptics said, but this is an illusion. Determinism asserts that human beings have no free will because we are particles, no more or less than everything else in the universe.

Four centuries ago human beings would have scoffed at the idea of determinism. But in the Age of Science, as mystery yielded to discovery, it became hard to argue against the concept that the material world functions according to immutable scientific laws. Why should we presume that human beings are able to override these laws and influence the matter and force of which we are made?

Determinism as a philosophy is strong evidence of the human tilt toward the world and away from the spirit. But there may be a tilting back. In the twentieth century science itself raised doubts about determinism. The discovery of relativity showed that time and space are not absolutes; quantum physics disproved the idea that anything is absolutely predictable. The universe may appear to function as if by clockwork, but at its outer dimensions and in its innermost workings, physical reality is inherently chaotic. The discovery of chaos underlying and overlaying the world has made scientific thinking more open to mystery, setting the stage for peaceful coexistence and possibly reconciliation between science and religion.

We know intuitively that we have free will. We experience ourselves considering decisions in context and considering the implications. Self awareness — *I* observing *me* with perspective — makes this experience possible. The perspective that enables awareness of oneself in a greater setting is the foundation of free will and responsibility.

Having the ability to perceive ourselves as part of the whole makes it possible to respond to fear and desire with the guidance of principle. We are able to exceed ourselves because we have selves. The self creates the possibility of moral choice.

I desire to buy a luxurious new car. Because I see myself in context I can stand aside from my desire and weigh the implications in the immediate sense and in the greater sense of myself as one drop in the water of existence. Is a luxurious new car the right use of resources given my desire for a life that has meaning? Are other people depending on me to use my resources for other purposes? What is my duty to them? Does the world need these resources? What is my duty to the world? Will I be using a disproportionate share of scarce fuel? Will I contribute to air pollution? If I must borrow to buy the car how will the burden of debt affect my ability to make moral choices in my professional life? Will the car own me?

These questions are not burdens imposed by moralistic thinking but questions that arise naturally from self-awareness and enable me to stay on course to meaning. *What is good in the long run for me?* is rarely if ever different from *What is good for all?* The concept of duty, which seems dreary and burdensome, aligns individual and collective interest. Duty may frustrate impulse, but duty gives the edge over time to the one who is self-aware. Duty is prepared to sacrifice short-run desire to secure long-run meaning.

We cannot necessarily know what is best for the self or for the whole. We are, however, able to go about making decisions in the right way, doing our best to be true to ourselves as participants in the systemic unity. In the aggregate and over time humanity will do what is best for the whole by seeking the truth of duty in the moment.

I desire one person, but I have promised fidelity to another. I want to become rich, but I also want to be a good spouse, parent and citizen. I want to build a house on a ridge over the canyon, but the building will change the vista.

Laying off employees will increase my firm's profits, but I feel loyal to my employees and I am concerned about the burden on the employees left behind. The standard justification for lay-offs is that all benefit because the workers will move on to more productive employment. What about the trauma of job loss? In the short term, lay-offs will increase the firm's earnings, but what are the long-term interests of the business? Would it be better served by my employees' having confidence in my loyalty to them? My own compensation will increase as profits follow from these lay-offs. How should I weigh my self-interest against the other interests involved? What about the quality of the firm's products and services? They may decline, but what are we in business for, quality or profit?

Among all these competing realities, what is my duty?

An understanding of duty can be enhanced by principles articulated in moral philosophy and religion as well as by cultural norms. Principle can create an elevating systemic relationship with the self. Attempting to act according to wise traditions may lead to an authentic understanding of what is right. But ultimately the self must be part of the process, taking responsibility for its own comprehension of right and wrong.

Competing principles must be resolved. Individual freedom must be reconciled with communal need. Laws and rules tend to infringe upon one to serve the other. If I am always on the side of individual rights, I can hardly learn about myself; nor can I learn about myself if I am always on the side of communal needs. Recognizing the coexistence and legitimacy of both, the conversation that takes place within me yields not a right answer but a heightened awareness. The idea that there is a right answer is an illusion. Seeking the answer in the right way is the answer.

In the conversational frame I have concerns about friendships, parenthood, professional relationships and human encounters from marriage to the street person who asks me for money. Aware of my fears and desires, I stand aside from myself and evaluate the situation in light of my short-term urges and long-term ideals. Often they are in accord. When they differ choosing in favor of the long term and the whole requires something of me that transforms me, as I am hardwired by instinct to choose the short-term and self-centered.

How many of our casual jokes and off-hand expressions excuse human failure to rise above ourselves! *Boys will be boys.* The idea of the fallen nature of humankind can be a blank check for mediocrity. *You can't teach an old dog new tricks.* We conspire to excuse our unwillingness to exercise free will and change. *That's just the way things are.*

In small bites each such denial makes little difference; cumulatively the failure to rise above ourselves portends cataclysm and possibly the end of humanity. We can understand human failings, but we cannot afford to rest from the work of trying to overcome them.

The exercise of free will creates capacity in the self. The pursuit of duty raises the volume of principle in the conversation. We become better able to stretch toward the ideal. This enhancement gives meaning and is progress across the arc of life from fear to love.

Love and Opening

Transition across the arc of life means surpassing the desire to prosper and the need to survive. The passage puts an end to the personal suffering created by fear and desire. And it puts an end to the stimulation of fear and desire in others. Crossing the arc of life heals the discontinuity in human systems and ends the perception of scarcity that causes violence.

The quality of human experience joins hands systemically with the quality of the world to create existence. Existence ascends as we change ourselves, moving past results orientation to a conversation between fear and love and ultimately to the surrender of fear to love. Then we may step across the inevitable threshold, not as losers in the struggle against death but as souls returning home.

The spirit carries us beyond ourselves, connecting our individual experience to others. The spirit moves us to relationship; to say hello to the stranger in a toll booth, to comfort the one who suffers, to become friends or lovers or partners in marriage. The spirit moves us to listen to the rolling ocean waves, to sit meditatively in a garden, to wonder at the waxing and waning of the moon. The spirit embraces the beautiful and spurs creation. The spirit hangs in there with us and coaxes and reassures and gives us strength to choose with integrity. The spirit can elevate us to give up life for another, to give up life for principle, to give up life when the body falls away.

The spirit is not about how to obtain results. The spirit influences what we do, but upstream where truth resides. The spirit is a countervailing system, not because it works against success in the world but because it leads the individual away from the fear and desire that require worldly success and toward sufficiency as a state of being.

In fear we act from a sense that we are isolated; in love from a sense that we are indivisible from the whole. Virtues like loyalty, honesty, gentleness, fairness, generosity, courage, respect, civility and humility are not only admirable but inevitable in the unity that comes from the spirit.

As the spirit moves restlessly into the world, it acquires and bestows the force of love. A raindrop falls in a lake and becomes the lake. As the spirit grows, blame and competition yield to acceptance and generosity. The world feeds back into the spirit but the spirit is first: aboriginal, epicentric, the source of change.

The seed of a soul resides in human life. Its potential is realized as the spirit moves energetically outward to systemic relationship with others, in friendship, family, society and the experience of unity. Miraculously, the greater the soul's experience of unity, the greater the soul's experience of individuality. This individuality is neither fearful nor separating but a creative individuality that conjoins and continues in its own way. The seed of a soul contains the potential to experience existence as one, as a raindrop in the lake. We are the lake and unique within it.

All is at hand. We find what we seek. In fear we find what we fear, in love we find what we love. I create my enemies with my fear. They are not imaginary. I create them because of the fear I exude.

Nature makes me aware of how my fearful efforts to be safe place me in peril. I went hiking where there were bears and I feared an encounter. I purchased pepper spray to defend myself. Possessing the spray did not allay my fears; it put me on the defensive and made me wary and cautious. What had been an open exploration of the natural world became a hunt. I came around a bend in the trail where the forest opened into a small clearing and there I confronted a bear standing on her hind legs shaking her head and moaning. As I stood there nervous and isolated I realized that my fear was causing her distress.

As we struggle through life we feel we must survive and we would like to prosper. Our felt need to survive and our desire to prosper can be satisfied only by capturing and exploiting resources for our own bene-fit. Some must win and some must lose; fear and desire increase.

The question of resources is not answered by an inventory of the world but by an inventory of existence. The quality of the world and the quality of human experi-ence merge systemically as existence. In this light, enough is not only a sense of enough, which could be false, and not only a quanti-ty of enough, which is bound to change. The vibrant self confluent with the living world creates, simply, enough.

I receive more than I release. When I grasped love I lost it and when I loosened my grip love appeared. Success eluded me until I stopped striving for it. Suffering made me understand life as unnecessary and death as a welcoming home. I do not mean that the lover who left returned or that fame and fortune appeared as I had hoped; and I did not become convinced that when we die we go to heaven. I found the significance and sufficiency beneath my worldly yearnings when I gave up grasping and striving and hoping.

The lens fell out of my glasses and I realized the tiny screw had come out of the frame. I was driving and I had no idea where the screw might have fallen. Angry at the injustice I felt and afraid of being alone without my glasses, I devised plans to search for the screw on the floor of the car, at the place I had parked and where I had been walking. Then I realized that I would be looking for something so small that finding it would be impossible. My thinking turned. I accepted that I could get along well enough without my glasses; all things considered they were rather unimportant. I gave up my anxious plans, resolving to have a look but releasing the outcome. I glanced down and there was the tiny screw in a wrinkle on my pant leg.

When I am at peace I can see how my life has unfolded in patterns. I am able to understand the present in light of the past. The world rearranges itself to accommodate what I desire deeply and know I do not need. I am filled with gratitude by something I once took for granted.

My friend begins to tell me about a painful experience. I hear just a few words and know as completely as I will know when the whole story is told.

A spiritual person tells me that a time of excitement and accomplishment lies ahead for me. I neither believe nor disbelieve and the time comes. My openness creates the other's clairvoyance.

In fear we make judgments in black and white. But human beings are poetic and prosaic, loving and fearful, compassionate and violent. We are light and shadow made flesh. We struggle to move toward the light, but our acknowledgement of the shadow in ourselves and others is wisdom.

In love there is no assessing others. We accept that some people are capable of choice and others are not. We see those capable of choice as fortunate, and we aspire to enhance our own capacity to choose. Our knowledge frees us from the prison of blame and the violence it incites.

As we open our eyes to reality, releasing

the false security of our illusions, we see in unity. We accept the pain in pleasure, the sorrow in joy, the dark danger in the beautiful. We understand that to receive is to give, to lose is to find, to know is to accept not-knowing, to gain is to let go. We learn the false distinction between subject and object, appreciating that what we own also owns us, that our destroying will destroy us, and that our loving loves us. We begin to take the enormous risk of premising our lives not upon hope but upon openness, going about life in conversation between instinct and principle, attempting to discern and carry out our duty. We solve problems increasingly within. As we accept the weakening and falling away of what can be seen, we embrace what we cannot see. We cease grasping and let go.

The miracle is that in acquiring the self, we leave the chains of the self behind. When it is, in fact, all about me — when I am engaged in an active, vibrant, energetic, creative, emerging self — I am sufficient unto myself, do not require your approval, do not need to control you and can love you in a way that helps you become yourself, even if it means losing you. There is a chance of losing you but there is no risk: sufficiency is there with or without you.

There is no direction to love. The distinction between loving and being loved is artificial. There are moments when one realizes that all one wants is to love the other, requiring nothing. There are moments of neither needing nor desiring to love the other — loving merely, the self falling away completely.

We want the human project to continue. We care deeply and compulsively. Because we are results-oriented we see a problem and immediately start thinking about what to do, and we start doing. Our well-intended efforts are beneficial or harmful or irrelevant. They fall short of moving systems to sustained ascendancy. We try harder or abandon our efforts in despair.

The world will get better when we stop needing it to get better. There will be clarity and right action when we are sufficient unto ourselves. Then we will be able to understand what the mystics mean when they say *All is well.*

Part III
Practice

Practice

Living in the right way is simple, but the world in which living must take place is complex. Because humanity has not lived in the right way the world is not right for living in that way. Instead of being uplifted by elevating systems and an evolving systemic unity, we are sculpted by influences of fear that create fear. We struggle and existence declines. We own the decline and the decline owns us.

What is becoming clear is that the way we struggle to get through our lives not really knowing ourselves — tragic at the individual level — is leading us *en masse* to a disaster that tragedy fails to describe. Intervention is required. What would that intervention look like?

The intervention would come from the individual, summoning the energy that remains in the spirit and stepping courageously, if cautiously, off the world's carousel. It would mean adopting practices designed to find meaning and to energize the spirit. It would mean progressing to a way of living in which these practices were integrated within the self, in order to sustain the hard work of realizing the self.

It would mean that people, wherever they are — not roaming the desert or seeking enlightenment on a mountain top — would become practitioners of the self.

The self is the locus of change. Practice of the self is a way of living that calls upon the immense power of free will. In practice of the self one goes about living in the world attending to its practical requirements but in conversation with the moral compass of the self.

Practice stokes the fire of the self, which warms the soul and energizes the individual to make the exhausting journey when external forces are aligned in opposition.

The Practice of Solitude

Solitude as practice is a response to the end of silence.

Silence on its own, an aboriginal and universal condition, was a void without meaning. Words were carved out of silence. For centuries words stood in contrast to and conversed with silence, one giving meaning to the other.

Now the noise of incessant verbiage, machinery and hurry has smothered silence. The conversation between words and silence has ended. The task of solitude is to overcome the disease of noise by willfully creating a silent space in which word — the essentially human characteristic and manifestation — can be resurrected and infused anew with meaning.

One can absent himself from the company of others and fail to achieve solitude. One may go to the woods to be alone, but the unending noise continues in the mind and peaceful surroundings do not afford the desired calm. True solitude is the equivalent of peace and sufficiency. The ability to experience depends upon the ability to be still, which is practiced in solitude. Solitude itself depends upon the ability to separate from the noise of the world. Few can achieve this state without constant practice.

Solitude nurtures a community of the self, a learning relationship between *I* and *me*. The person in whom *I* and *me* exist in relationship is introspective without being self-conscious. The self is to be observed and explored as is. There is no need to make and remake a *faux* self. Introspection in this regard is for the conjoining of *I* and *me*, not the remaking of *me* by *I*.

Introspection is by definition reflective and investigative, not obsessive. The developed self is also capable of concluding the introspection and moving on.

The practices of solitude move the self toward the relationship in which all is lost and thereby gained.

Being Alone

Crowded lives make us lonely. We try to solve the problem of loneliness by attaching ourselves to other people. We seek romance or friendship in order to find a substitute for the lonely, diminished self. The practice of solitude requires that the problem of loneliness be solved not by surrounding ourselves with others but by learning how to be alone. Solitude as practice requires first that, although one may seek freely the company of others, one must not do so in order to assuage the pain of loneliness.

When the only reason for wanting to be with others is the avoidance of being alone, the practitioner resists and faces himself. The other practices of solitude make it possible at first — and later rewarding — to be alone.

Meditation

Consciousness intervenes in the conjunction of *I* and *me*. Action, thought, memory, imagination, will and emotion create diversions. The practice of meditation suspends these diversions and allows a person simply to be. In the meditative state *I* and *me* flow together naturally, undistracted by the normal static of the mind.

Meditation is difficult for the revved-up personality and perhaps for that reason has been accorded an esoteric status it does not deserve. A person meditates by clearing the mind, freeing himself from the constant burden of thought. Like a child learning how to float in a swimming pool, the mind must be trained to be still and to let go of struggling. The mind rests for a second, then wants to spring back into action. In meditation one is patient with this child but gently insistent that it return to stillness until the allotted period — measured in seconds at first and then extending with practice to minutes — is over.

Various devices such as mantras — repeated words or phrases — can be employed, as can special breathing and stretching exercises. There are many approaches to meditation and many books have been written about it. But meditation is not arcane and inaccessible.

Meditation can be undertaken without assuming the lotus position and without esoteric technique. My morning practice begins with simple stretching, a routine derived from lower back exercises I have been doing for many years. As I lie on my back and pull my knees to my chest, I count 20 slow breaths, in and out, to time the stretch. I have five such stretches, during which I want not only to exercise my lower back muscles but to begin relieving the incessant thinking of my restless mind, which starts up as soon as I awaken. Then, when the temperature is not too cold and the wind not too high, I take my pillow and a warm blanket outside, place the pillow on the edge of my porch facing the mountains and take my seat upon the pillow, crossing my legs and resting my feet on the first step down off my porch. I am not flexible enough to cross my legs comfortably on the level where I am sitting, but I do like the feeling of crossed legs. I am deliberate and careful in my movements, as if placing the cushion, taking my seat and wrapping the blanket around my shoulders were a ritual — a repeated series of movements with intrinsic significance. When the weather is too harsh for a peaceful meditation, I follow a version of this routine inside my house using several cushions and sitting in a peaceful place near my wood stove.

When I am settled outside I gaze out upon the new day and become aware of where I am and what my purpose is. I want to relieve my mind of its undisciplined jitterbugging from one subject to another and reassert my own influence, reaching an accommodation in which focus and creativity can be partners. Much as in the act of pulling the blanket around my shoulders, I pull a shroud of calm and silence around my mind, not forcing it to be quiet but allowing it to calm down to a peaceful, unspecific awareness. I use my breath to give my mind a focal point. When my mind asserts itself and sneaks off to plan or remember or fantasize, I pull it gently back to my breath. When my timer tells me that my chosen time has passed or when I simply feel that my meditation has ended, I take stock, asking what the quality of the experience tells me about the state of my mind and spirit.

I recommend committing to the practice of meditation over a period of time — say five mornings a week for three months — without any expectation of noticeable results. Find a place and time in which uninterrupted quiet can be assured, sit cross-legged on the floor or in a comfortable, straight-backed chair. If you choose a chair, rest your feet flat upon the floor and place your hands on your legs or in your lap. Gaze downward at something relatively unspecific like a spot on the floor or the point at which a table leg meets the carpet. Gaze — don't focus — and release yourself from thinking. Float into not-thinking and remain there lightly for as long as you can without artificial forcing, which is thought. Notice your surroundings, but incidentally, as one notices a breeze on a perfect spring day. When thoughts appear, welcome them and let them go. Pass them on through the exit door of your experience and restore yourself to solitude.

Do this for two minutes per meditation in the first week, then add minutes in succeeding weeks. I reiterate the importance of having no expectation; this is essential. Beginning meditation will not alter your life nor bring you to nirvana. You probably will feel frustrated and perhaps conclude that meditation doesn't work for you. Meditation is like distance running: its rewards must be earned over time. Meditation requires discipline and patience. If you practice meditation faithfully for three months you may find peace, focus, purpose, clarity, acceptance or something else unexpected. You will then be able to decide whether meditation is for you or not.

Contemplation of Beauty

Another practice of solitude is contemplation of beauty. The beautiful may be found in many places and forms. In choosing what to contemplate recognize that beauty is a demanding essence. What is attractive is not necessarily beautiful. The contemplation of beauty is an active response to beauty's demand. Much of what is attractive or even compelling may not make a good subject for contemplation because nothing is demanded.

Poetry surprises and beckons the reader to think and feel. Classical music attracts not with words but with abstract, evocative sounds. An impressionist painting is poetry as nonverbal image.

The object of contemplation invites the observer to consider. What are the implications of a delicate flower? What does its perfection tell us about our own nature? How was this common yet intricate thing designed? Why must it wilt? What does its eventual death mean for this moment in which it exists, fragrant and colorful?

Contemplation is participation in a conversation. To contemplate is to bring sensation through the conscious mind and into the unconscious.

As with any practice, contemplation requires a degree of sophistication developed by learning and repeated experience. To appreciate Bach it is helpful to understand classical music forms. To know an orchid it is helpful to something about varieties of orchids. But knowledge is not contemplation. Contemplation is both passive and active. The contemplator engages the object, is open to what it communicates and brings his own message to the process. My contemplation of a flower is as unique as my conversation with a friend.

What appeals to you? What does your intuition tell you that you want to know about and be with? Set aside a period of time — a year perhaps — in which to learn and develop the ability to converse with the kinds of beauty that engage you. The person who contemplates develops the ability over time to lose himself in the contemplation.

Making a Journal

Making a journal is a process like meditation or contemplation. The point of a journal is not the written product but the writing process. A journal may refer to what one has done or plans to do but should not be thought of as a record. In making a journal the practitioner depicts the self in order to learn about the self.

Human beings are nothing so much as what they feel. The journalist writes extensively about emotions, those he is feeling at the moment and those he has felt. Journals are excellent for the recording of dreams and fantasies. So much is repressed within us. The problem with repression is not necessarily keeping emotions and visions from others but keeping them from ourselves. Making a journal heightens awareness of the hidden self.

The practice of going within is well accomplished in the gentle discipline and routine of keeping a journal. Often I notice nothing in particular about myself until I pick up my journal to determine what I have to say about and to myself that morning. I write in my journal every morning and at other times when I feel a need for focused introspection. Disciplined routine creates significance. Frequently there ensues a flood of information about feelings, dreams and reflections on experience. As I write I consider more deeply and carefully what is true about me. In engraving the writing on the page, I engrave my thoughts and emotions upon my awareness.

I recommend choosing an appealing journal book. Do you like the cover? Do you like the texture of the pages? Is the paper thick enough? Do you prefer lined or unlined paper? Can you befriend and trust the book? Ask the same kinds of questions about the pen or pencil you will use. When you have found the right writing instrument, stay with it. Make it a partner of your journal and an extension of your hand.

The purpose of making a journal is making the journal. The journal should not be thought of as something to publish or pass on to one's heirs or as a record to be read by anyone else. There must be no posturing in a journal. A journal is a private conversation and should be kept in a private place.

Contemplation of Words

I begin my day with a routine of stretching, listening to music, writing in my journal and reading from a text.

The self-realization I seek in my morning ritual benefits from the wisdom in a text whose words are dense and poetic, conducive to the contemplation of truth. Scriptural texts — from the Hebrew and Christian Bibles or the Hindu *Bhagavad Gita* — are common choices. There is a wealth of beautiful text — some of it concrete prose, some of it poetic and mystical — in the writings of the great religions.

I take these rich documents in small bites, savoring each according to my capacity that day. I want the words to help open me with their beauty and wisdom. Also, my openness enhances their beauty and wisdom. To the receptive mind any such text is sufficient to promote spiritual experience. Contemplation is a systemic relationship with the text that begins with the knowing of the mind and moves it to the unknowing of the spirit.

But one must begin the contemplation of words where one is, intellectually and spiritually. My morning reading has included many books that would appear to have little spiritual content but were necessary to get my mind in shape so that I could move past my mind to the spirit. I have read books in the morning that were essentially scientific or sociological. The important thing in these writings was that the wisdom of the authors created an aura of truth beyond the narrow focus of the book. The writings of the biologist E. O. Wilson and the psychologist Karen Horney are among these.

Works of philosophy, especially those

written for the average reader, also have attracted me. A small but powerful book called *Man's Search for Meaning*, written by the psychoanalyst and concentration camp survivor Viktor Frankl, was one of these. *The World of Silence*, by the existential and mystical philosopher Max Picard, was another. Contemporary books that describe scientific revelations such as relativity and quantum physics in light of religion and philosophy have been another source of wisdom and inspiration. Older writings such as the Platonic dialogues that describe the trial and death of Socrates and Wordsworth's autobiographical poem, "The Prelude" were also important sources.

The important thing is to pick a text that speaks to you where you are. Read it in small bites. Re-read it if you feel like it. Work with it, making notes in the margins and underlining if you wish.

In my early days of practice no writing was more influential than a collection of letters and essays of Mahatma Gandhi. I recall vividly the night that this book found me. I was browsing in a bookstore attempting to distract myself from turmoil in my personal life. I had no intention of pursuing Gandhi, but his voice was like a father's voice, firm but soft, demanding but comforting. Lincoln's voice has the same effect on me, especially the voice that speaks in his letters.

I favor books that ask something of me and books written in simple words without allusions to esoteric things. I like books that speak humbly.

It is important to find words that invite you. Go to a bookstore or library trusting that the right book will find you. Take your time. Don't make finding a book a necessary outcome. Sometimes you must come away without one.

Prayer

Prayer and meditation flow in and out of my morning process. For example, recounting an emotion in my journal often turns into a reflection on how I am going about an aspect of my life, such as a relationship or a work project. The reflection becomes a realization that I must change, and then becomes a prayer as I seek the strength to do the essential work of changing — not the world but myself.

The practices of solitude do not require prayer to take place but promote and allow it. Prayer is multifarious and subjective. I find that I pray best, realizing the presence of God, when my experience becomes prayer without my willing it or even knowing it at first. I simply allow myself to flow into prayer. I pray within a presence not called upon by my prayer but recognized by it.

Those well practiced in prayer initiate it and engage in it according to their preference in the moment. Kinds of prayer include ritualistic and repetitive prayer, petitioning prayer, confessional or self-revealing prayer and silent prayer.

Prayer is self-expressing and self-enhancing. Prayer is self-forgetting. Prayer is a microcosm of the journey across the arc of life, from the inner reaches of the self, so the self may be realized, so the self may ultimately be transcended. Encountering God is self-encountering no matter how the discourse takes place.

For those not well versed in prayer I recommend patience. Prayer will come if you give it room. Allow God to break through to you. And you must forgive yourself for not praying, which is itself a kind of prayer.

Radical Introspection

The specific practices of solitude lead to radical introspection. Habitual and rigorous self-examination is fostered by the practices of solitude and by living with those practices as priorities, as integrated as the practice of a profession or parenthood or retirement or any other way of life. Radical introspection refers to the custom of looking below the surface of one's action and thought to examine motivation and consider whether action is consistent with belief.

Do I wish to reach out because I want to be with that person or because I want to avoid being alone? My desire to help someone may seem motivated by generosity, but my helpful inclinations may reflect my need for approval or my desire to make another person dependent on me. Am I angry? Am I aware of my anger or am I responding to familial and cultural messages that I should not "get angry"? Is my suppression likely to cause me to lash out violently at someone else or myself? Am I afraid? Are my plans consistent with my beliefs? Are my actions consistent with my plans? What lies behind my justifications and explanations? Am I being too hard on myself? Not hard enough?

In radical introspection I attend to myself and create myself each day from the ground up. My introspection is radical not because it is outside social boundaries but because it is at the very center of my being. Radical introspection is life lived as prayer.

The Practice of Truth

We are driven to perceive *truth* as we are driven to find and create selves. The will to the self, the will to meaning and the will to truth are post-survival extensions of the will to survive. In an impermanent existence we long for something lasting and unchanging. We are meant to strive for the truth.

But we must do so within the framework of human limitation. We are born in fear and must struggle to move past it. Conspiracies of pretense and dissembling prevail in a fearful and complacent society. Social conventions preserve ways of knowing that preclude the truth, and the lie is becoming the conventional truth. Living truthfully requires intense effort. The pursuit of unchanging truth as the centerpiece of life is extraordinary.

The practice of truth involves honesty and learning.

Untruthful utterances are violent and self-defeating. Practitioners of truth speak as honestly as they can. They have no desire to disrupt the flow of conventional dialogue, but they avoid saying that they are fine if they are not fine. They attempt to answer in ways that do not disconcert others and do not require dishonesty. They do not endorse the shibboleth "white lie." They do not fabricate, exaggerate or understate. They do not offer judgments gratuitously, but if they are asked and decide to answer, they do so responsibly and truthfully.

The truthful value their words as they value themselves. Honesty leaves open the question of how the other will respond. For this reason honesty evidences and advances self-sufficiency. Honesty releases control and requires courage. It is self-reliance in that practitioners treat what they perceive, recall, feel or believe, as enough — not enough for the other but enough for themselves — to sustain them in the face of an unpredictable response.

The child who grows up in a family in which honesty is the rule receives a gift more valuable than the most elaborate university education. Others must overcome early experience. An essential role of a mentor is to assist the student in practicing honesty.

The vows that deal with human interaction — truth, nonviolence and service — all raise questions about extreme situations. Practical questions with philosophical implications arise occasionally: What should the dying patient be told? Is it better to be honest and betray a comrade or to lie and protect him? Universal maxims are perilous; hard cases require practitioners to make choices where there is no clear answer.

Openness is sometimes confused with honesty. That I have been asked a question does not necessarily mean that I must answer it. If your shirt does not match your tie or if you are becoming forgetful or your politics are inferior to mine, it does not necessarily mean that I must tell you so. One who commits to speak honestly must discriminate in deciding whether to speak at all.

It is possible to learn, to become more aware of the coexistence of the mutually exclusive, more accepting of ambiguity, more suspicious of one's own limitations, and more alert to the inadequacy and treachery of words. It is possible to experience truth even though it does not come in easy and convenient packages.

Truth has no equivalent except in words that also describe what is at once simple and complex, such as love, unity and God. In life we cannot know truth literally, but we can know that truth exists and we can know aspects of truth.

Perspective is an important aspect of truth. Immersed in fear, I lack perspective because I lack information, wisdom, and tragic awareness; I lack the mystical sense that all is one. These are crucial stages in attaining a truthful perspective. They describe another way of understanding the arc of life: from fear to love, from ignorance to truth.

The search for truth is disappointing, difficult and dangerous. The fear of truth makes us cling to our slogans and limits our ability to learn. Ignorance is the oxygen of fear. It feeds the inability and unwillingness to learn. Fear interacts with ignorance, one sponsoring the other in a devolving cycle. How do we deal with the inability to rid the mind of bias, to see in wholes, to pierce the veil of conventional untruth?

We learn about what is and what has been so we can recognize patterns. We acquire greater perspective from experience and introspection, which expand the frames we see through and enhance our sense of implication, as well as our sense of humor. We observe and learn to accept that opposite qualities inhere in all worldly phenomena: that judgments about good and evil rarely go far enough; that the world is but change itself; and that worldly truth is an illusion.

The reversal of existential spirals would require humankind to make the practice of truth not incidental to living but living incidental to the practice of truth. Truth as practice means moving away from the darkness of ignorance to the light of knowledge, wisdom, acceptance of the unsafe and irreconcilable, and embracing the unknowable.

Form a relationship with yourself through radical introspection. Be vigilant to your feelings, question the validity of your perceptions and converse with yourself to assess your responses. Learn about the world around you as you learn about yourself. Approach life with curiosity, as someone always beginning to learn.

Treat every utterance as valuable. Use words sparingly. Speak humbly and sincerely. Question yourself constantly.

Aspire to truth as artists aspire to beauty, as physicians labor against death, as sprinters race against time.

The vibrant self can reverse the decline in the quality of existence. We are free to choose truth. And we have, over the course of our long lifetimes, the potential

to encounter aspects of truth — to make
progress — so that death is a mere footstep over the threshold of truth.

The Practice of Nonviolence

Nonviolence is loaded with connotation, a marginal word used by and about people who have threatened the established order. Many of its exemplary practitioners have been assassinated. This tells us much about the power of nonviolence. Why were those in power threatened by the gentlest of people?

Nonviolence springs from awareness of the wholeness of the living world. The practitioner of nonviolence perceives the world not as a hostile environment in which he must attack and defend but as one of continuity and interdependence. The practitioner is aware of consequence and implication. Nonviolence means doing no harm and more. Nonviolence is love in practice. Nonviolence is loving one's neighbor *as* oneself, in the sense that one's neighbor *is* oneself.

Violence is the irresponsible assertion of one's will. There is obvious violence, to which we are obviously addicted. There is subtle violence, in which we are immersed and do not see, as a fish is unaware of water. The most common and dehumanizing violence is hurry, in which we rush from thought to thought, action to action and place to place. We bemoan hurry as if we have no choice but to submit. In fact we do have a choice but we don't want the burden of choosing. Our hurry pushes and provokes others to hurry in order to do our will, get their fair share, oppose us outright or get out of our way. In their turn others act in ways that frighten us and compel us to hurry.

The twentieth century witnessed a profusion of technology intended to make work more efficient, but at the close of the century we were far more harassed by our own impatience than at the start. In our hurry the hours, days and seasons fly by and the practices of solitude and truth seem less relevant and become marginal. As process yields to results, authenticity vanishes and relationships decline and violent thought yields violent action.

The practitioner of nonviolence perceives the world not as a hostile environment in which he must attack and defend but as one of continuity and interdependence. The practitioner of nonviolence is gentle and patient in a world of harshness and speed. Patience values the self. Patiently, I value my experience and allocate my time thoughtfully. I favor the conversation between the results I want — *How do I get everything done today?* — and the quality I seek in living this day — *How do I want to live?*

Nonviolence includes nonviolent speech in tone and meaning. The nonviolent practitioner is polite and deferential in a world of incivility and aggression. Epithets, slurs and other offensive words are avoided, as are offensive gestures. Nonviolence precludes making noise gratuitously. Nonviolence supports listening over speaking. In a world of noise the practitioner's use of words is measured.

The nonviolent speaker has confidence in his words. He is kind, civil without being obsequious and pleasant in social interaction without being unduly superficial. Even a person with a gruff personality acquires an aura of gentleness in nonviolence.

Nonviolence avoids blaming. I take special pains here to differentiate between assessing circumstance and blaming people. Often it is useful to find out what happened in a particular situation so that it can be remedied, prevented from recurring and understood for the purposes of assigning legitimate consequences. When we blame we assess irresponsibly and offload responsibility from ourselves to others.

Consequences are legitimate when dealt out in an awareness of unity. But a true awareness of unity will cause the responsible individual to be aware of his own participation in every crime and his identity with every criminal.

In nonviolence consequence is followed by forgiveness, a return to the truth of unity. Forgiveness is not an erasure or a forgetting of wrongdoing but a recognition of continuing relationship. After forgiveness a relationship is not necessarily the same as before. The restored relationship may lack its former depth, or the hurt and forgiveness may give new depth to a formerly shallow relationship.

Punishment in anger and retribution, frequently carried out in the name of justice, is violent whether the punishment takes the form of physical violence or the passive ending of a relationship.

Nonviolence precludes striking and diminishing. I engage in unacceptable violence when I attack someone physically or speak to someone using a tone or words that separate that person from himself.

The practitioner does not avoid observing violence if circumstance requires it, but he avoids the celebration of violence.

Nonviolence precludes sadism and masochism. The nonviolent practitioner avoids the gratuitous use of weapons. He is not entertained by violence in sports and pornography nor by violence in movies and television.

It is impossible to exist without committing violence. As a practical matter my life depends upon my immune system's defending me against inimical living beings. The fact that I breathe, eat and take up space makes inevitable the death of other beings and contributes to the suffering of all beings. The nonviolent practitioner is aware that when he eats he is sustaining his life by the sacrifice of life.

There are many plausible arguments against nonviolence. Violence may have to be taken up in order to prevent harm. The practitioner of nonviolence departs from his practice with reluctance and with skepticism about his own motivation. He understands that to avoid violence is to grant himself a gift and that engaging in violence is a deprivation, perhaps one from which he may never fully recover. The practitioner of nonviolence realizes that to act violently toward another, no matter how justifiably, is to take a hatchet to his own soul.

We are addicted to having and doing, and our unbounded craving and possessiveness are kinds of violence. Ownership excludes and when ownership becomes hoarding, it harms. The person who hoards or wastes inflicts suffering. The deprivation is not only of the thing hoarded or wasted but of the self of the one who is hoarding or wasting.

The practitioner of nonviolence honors the process of competition as defined by its rules and traditions. He considers the goal of winning within his own sense of right and wrong. The practitioner may compete ardently but does not allow himself to become morally separated from his competitor. He may take pleasure in winning but not in another's losing. His competing honors his opponent.

Nonviolence is a personal doctrine, not a political one. Nonviolent resistance has been effective in the reversal of such violent spirals such as colonialism and racism because it has enabled the powerful to experience their own suffering.

The nonviolent practitioner teaches by example rather than by sermon. Public displays of nonviolence are not intended to be personal exhibitions. The nonviolent practitioner serves and gives. His interest is in attending to a problem rather than calling attention to himself.

Violence inflicts pain, sorrow and misery; it deprives human beings of meaning. Mass violence is the aggregate of small acts of violence by people like us. It is the collective manifestation of our poor relationships with ourselves, with each other and with the world as a whole.

It is possible to practice discreet acts of nonviolence and acquire a greater sense of, and commitment to, nonviolence as a way of life. Small actions of conservation and generosity lead to awareness of the wasting and hoarding that create massive suffering. If we refrain from violent reactions in traffic or on crowded sidewalks, we may begin to know the rewards of a new peace. If we break away from our addiction to violence in sports or other forms of entertainment, we may feel lost at first but later feel more tranquil and self-possessed. The reward in non-blaming is the burden and fulfillment of responsibility. Forgiveness brings about forgiveness, including self-forgiveness.

The nonviolent practitioner is an ideal to which those of us who are not saints can aspire. A monk or a nun can be violent and a cowboy or a corporate chieftain can practice nonviolence. You can be a teenager or an octogenarian, a big guy with a leather jacket or a glittering socialite. You can like hip-hop or elevator music. Your voice can be loud or soft, your personality that of an introvert or extrovert.

Commence the practice of nonviolence where you are. Have no preconception about what you might become and have no fear. Nothing can happen against your will. If you change it will be because you want to.

Reversing the declining condition of the systemic unity begins with the transformation of one person to nonviolence.

The Practice of Service

*S*ervice as practice emerges naturally from a loving conception of life. In the integrated life the quality of the process is inseparable from the quality of the accomplishment. Whereas fear and desire narrow the frames of perception and isolate result from process, love envisions the whole, inspires conversation between the pragmatic and ideal, and protects the continuity of systems. The servant practitioner is one who recognizes his interest as consistent with that of the world around him.

Service is an attitude. It is possible to work as a volunteer feeding the hungry without serving. It is also possible to work as an investment banker and serve. When work is performed as service the self does its work of extending beyond the individual to the world. For the practitioner truth is the aspiration, nonviolence is the ethos and service is the frame of mind.

When I speak to a group or teach a class without making my desire for approval the focal point, I feel able to intuit the reactions of audience members. I know when the group needs more and when enough is enough. I know when a word of humor will help and when it will distract. I know when a break is needed or when a question needs to be asked. I do not feel that I must control the teaching and learning exclusively but that I can collaborate with my students. Serving gives me confidence in myself, my students and the teaching-learning process.

When my efforts have been in service, I find them sufficient to themselves. The desire for compensation and appreciation and the fear of rejection become submerged in the experience. When I have served I experience enough. When I have worked but not served I remain needy.

For whom do I work as an employee? Am I focused on impressing my boss or on serving my boss, my colleagues, my subordinates, my firm and its customers? How do I carry out my duties as a manager? Do I see myself as the servant of the colleagues over whom I have authority? Do I consider it my job to serve my subordinates by teaching them what I expect and providing the resources and motivation to deliver? Can I encourage them to perform at a level that may exceed my own achievements? Is my aim to establish my importance in the reflected glory of my subordinates? Can I forgive them when they fail and feel genuine satisfaction when they succeed and are recognized for their success without my receiving credit?

For whom do I work as a parent? Is my parenthood about my desire for the adoration of my children? Is it about their fulfilling my unrealized dreams? Am I able to relate to them so that their needs remain first in my mind? Am I able to maintain boundaries intended for my self-preservation and their moral development, even at the risk of their disapproval? Do I need them or, when the time is right, can I let them go? I ask similar questions of myself as a friend, a lover and a spouse.

Service is to the self even when it appears altruistic or sacrificial. Those recognized as saintly should be understood not as better than you and I but as people who have served themselves better than you and I do. Those who use violence to gain power and property may be seen as lost in spirals of self-destruction.

Service inspires. People do not expect to be served and are skeptical of service and those who serve them. Service may frighten people. But if the servant's motive is pure his attitude breaks through to the one being served like spring after a long winter. Service can turn an opponent into an ally. But the focal point of service must be to serve, leaving the one served free to choose his own course. Service requires courage because to serve you must go first.

The devolving systemic nature of our world pulls every human being toward irresponsibility, making service hard. This does not defeat the possibility of service; it elevates the necessity. The corporate lawyer may serve the cause of truth as much as the nun. The lawyer need not resign his law practice to serve. He can decline to misrepresent and misuse the legal system, a constituency he must serve as surely as he serves his client. He may have to risk losing the associations that depended on his former willingness to short-change himself, but ultimately he will realize that those associations were superfluous and detrimental. He will win himself and gain respect and power he never anticipated, if he has the courage to serve.

The servant will be pressured to abandon his attitude of service. The one who serves threatens the established order, especially if he cannot be ignored. Almost certainly he will subject to seduction or attack.

The practice of service itself provides the confidence, light-heartedness and humor to overcome the violent and the seductive.

The Practice of Intended Uses

The practice of *intended uses* begins with an acceptance that what one receives — be it a material possession, a personal characteristic, a relationship or an experience of any kind — is a gift. Within every gift is a purpose. The practice of intended uses means accepting and attempting to make use of what has been given according to the intention inherent in the gift. Illness, confusion, bankruptcy, the departure of a loved one — occurrences that bring about suffering — contain an intended purpose, as do a rewarding friendship or a winning lottery ticket.

It is my duty to refrain from causing others to suffer and my duty to help ease suffering, but in suffering there is an opportunity to learn about the capacity for enduring without yielding principle. Even something so universally desired as inherited wealth may bring suffering, as in shame and isolation or being deprived of the opportunity of struggle.

The concept of intended uses applies as well to all the good things and gifts we tend to want: intelligence, beauty, wealth, stature, even physical health and life itself. We may enjoy any of these, but intended uses requires that we not treat them as unconditional entitlements. Intended uses requires that we use what is given according to its purpose as best we can divine it.

I am given food each day, far more than I need. Food is intended to sustain my life and fuel my body to perform well. I also believe that food is given for occasions of enjoyment and community. On the other hand I believe that eating to avoid an unpleasant feeling, like loneliness, guilt, anxiety or anger, is not intended in the gift of food. Intended uses requires me to use food for health and communal enjoyment and to refrain from eating in order to change my mood.

Trying to divine intended uses seems daunting. Can there be an infallible road map leading to a perfect life? Have no such illusion. The question is not whether you get it right but whether you are trying to get it right. Intended uses is the practice of wondering and attempting to discern.

Life makes sense in retrospect. Patterns push us toward a destiny that reveals itself over time. In the short run we must go about living as though feeling our way along a path at night, footstep by footstep. Signposts guide us without giving the big picture. Talent is one of these guiding signals. We are hard-wired with talent, and we are given clues about our talent, and perhaps our destiny, early in life. I have talent; what I am to do with it?

To what use shall I put a new relationship? Why is this person in my life? Use seems like a harsh and pragmatic word to describe a relationship, but we need not think of it as such. The intended use of a relationship may be my treating that person kindly without expecting to receive anything in return. I may learn to appreciate that the other person is loving me simply by receiving my kindness. Another may teach me outright about myself, or I may learn as I observe the way I treat the other person.

What use is intended in wealth? For one person the intended use may be to give wealth away to charity, to experience the contribution as a loss to the wallet, a gain to the self and a benefit to society. For another person the intended use may be to build a museum or maintain a home in which beauty is created or preserved. For another the intended use of wealth may be to make wise and productive investments.

We must consider our own wealth, inquiring why so much has been given to us, what responsibility it implies and what we are meant to explore and express with it.

At the center of intended uses is the virtue of humility, with the mystery that humility entails. In humility one pursues knowledge of the self without self-centeredness. In humility one acquires power by letting go of power. As infants and small children we saw power residing in people, places and things beyond us. In the practice of intended uses we acknowledge our inseparability from circumstance and seek knowledge of ourselves by knowing what surrounds us as well as what is within us. Intended uses is simply another side of radical introspection.

Under intended uses I let go of my sense of entitlement and my sense that what affects others has no relation to me. The practices of solitude, truth, nonviolence and service pull me under the tent of existence. Inside the tent it is possible to see everything that happens as having a purpose I am meant to honor. And there is no part of the tent in which I do not dwell.

Vows

The pressures of the world conspire forcefully against practice. From what source do we gain the power to become practitioners and sustain practice?

Several years ago I was living alone on a farm in an area where I had no family nearby, no intimate friend and no one who loved me or even knew me well. Friends and lovers had departed from me or I from them. I was profoundly bereft. I asked myself why I was doing the hard and painful work of living. I was not close to suicide but I considered why shouldn't I be?

I was fortunate that I had time to sit with my despair, to cry alone in anger and anguish about the wreckage of my life. It had been leveled. Should I rebuild it?

There was an intimacy in this aloneness. I took walks in the countryside where for once I could appreciate beauty without wanting to possess it. I read and fell in love with Gandhi, whose simple words seemed a kind of home. I returned to my old loves of music and poetry and experimented with new practices such as journal keeping and meditation. I thought about the important people in my life, alive and dead. I worked at reconstructing my past, not just looking for causes, as in therapy, but searching for patterns that gave meaning.

Since childhood I had experienced the strange phenomenon of a shivering chill when I was afraid. I would hear something in the night, my ears would tighten against my head like a horse in fear, and a chill at once horrifying and wonderful would come over me.

One dark night sitting alone near a window in the farmhouse, I looked up from my book and saw a distorted image of my own face in the warped glass of the window pane. The reflection was made grotesque by the flickering candle on the table next to me. A chill spread over me, but instead of turning away and dismissing my fear, I did not resist. I realized that I was, while having this shivering chill of terror, in the presence of God. I allowed myself to remain there.

I realize the presence of God when fear and love seem poised as on the edge of a knife. I feel the chill as I write today.

I was open in those days as I had never been before. My admiration and love of Gandhi led me to experiment with vows.

My experiments turned to practice, which turned into the centerpiece of my life.

I believe in the self and I believe in choice, and I believe in vows.

It is easy enough to see the value of practice in theory, but it is hard to reverse cycles: the way we live is the cycle we seek to reverse. To go against the tide we must go against ourselves as we are and emerge to become ourselves as we might be. *How can I intervene within myself and turn myself around?* There must be something aboriginal and extraordinary to get us from idea to practice and keep us there.

The word vow is in common usage today as a verb. When we say that someone vows to accomplish something, we mean that the person has made a serious statement of intention. The word is used less often as a noun. Religious practitioners make vows such as poverty, chastity and obedience. It is common for a bride and groom to express vows of fidelity during the wedding ceremony. We understand superficially what these vows require, but we do not comprehend what it actually means to make and keep a vow, incorporating it in the self.

Marital vows require monogamy. Monastic vows call for celibacy. Our understanding of these is superficial. We see them as white-knuckle restraints against red-blooded desire. But vows of monogamy and celibacy mean far more than limiting or eliminating sexual partners. Consider the magnitude of what marital and religious vows are intended to support. In marriage two people, separate in mind and body, aspire to become a single person in spirit. The monk and nun mean to detach themselves from the thrall of the world of which they are part and on which they depend. White-knuckling it might work for a time, but we are speaking of lifetimes. To accomplish their aspirations, marital partners and religious ascetics must evolve in spirit to become people for whom fidelity to one's partner or refraining from sex altogether are not unnatural but consistent, even inevitable. Their vows must not only restrain but transport them.

The actual subject matter of a vow is the self. Making a vow is a premeditated, comprehensive exercise of free will in which the self is transformed.

A vow is not a sincere expression of intention but a commitment of the whole person to a way of life. It goes beyond sincerity and resolve. Avowal means leaving one place in your life and moving to another place. Making a vow is like jumping off a cliff: you go beyond the point of no return. The distinction between sincere resolution and transformation is critical but subtle because in making a vow you are not literally jumping off a cliff. You can return to the point of avowal and get divorced or leave the priesthood. And no one who takes a profound vow is capable of living up to its demands at all times and in every respect.

But someone who has made a vow in fact has made a commitment in spirit so complete that he can no more return to the point of avowal than the cliff jumper can return to the jumping-off point. The vow, if actually made, turns the avower into a new person. The avower is no longer someone standing on firm ground but, having jumped, is in mid-air, off to a new and unknown destination.

Avowal is an intentional process in which someone begins as one person and emerges as another person, one who is guided by a higher principle. Instinct inevitably raises desires that challenge the vow, but the transformation places the avower in a different place with a new hierarchy of values and a new perspective. The vow creates a motivation opposed to and stronger than that of instinctive desire. In making a vow one does not merely say, *I have made a vow and now I must keep it*; one changes oneself into a new *I*, for whom keeping the vow is part of self-identity.

Making a vow involves months of preparation. I have not made a new vow in several years, but I require myself to practice any proposed vow for a year before I make it. I have made provisional vows and rejected them, almost always because I realized that they were covered by the vows I had already made.

In the provisional phase the vow is practiced as ardently as if it had been made as a final vow. This is essential to move the self to an awareness in which transformation is possible. I must be able to see myself in the practice of the vow. I have not made a life-changing commitment, and I do not attempt to carry the burden of a transformation before there actually has been one. A premature commitment creates pressure; transformation releases it. The provisional phase is training in thought, action and self-awareness, opening the door to profound change.

Making a resolution means that I sincerely want to behave differently. Making a vow means that I am different. A vow is not made only in the head with deliberation or in the heart with emotion; a vow is utterly radical, a voluntary reorientation of the self. The head may see the benefit of a way of living, the heart may desire it, but it cannot be a vow until the *I* of the self perceives and accepts *me* as one in whom the vow is embodied. This requires trial, practice and living unselfconsciously with the vow at the center.

It is never possible to effect a perfect and complete transformation. Where is the dividing line between intending a vow and making a vow? You may describe yourself as an avowed practitioner of nonviolence, but until your self-concept depends on not harming, you have not made the vow. You must move from acting nonviolently to being nonviolent.

The making of vows is a process that starts with an emergence from unawareness or denial. You may not see yourself as a violent person because you do not notice your hurry and disregard of people who slow you down. You do not notice your antagonism toward people with whom you compete for scarce resources. You do not notice your coldness when offended or the heat of your words when frightened. Something then comes into your awareness — an intervention occurs by happenstance or through a calamitous loss, leaving you no choice but to examine yourself from a fresh perspective. You become aware of the internal setting for violence that you impose on your external environment and you begin to consider nonviolence.

A vow calls out to you when you are in need. The first step is contemplating the vow, envisioning how it might influence your life and assessing what it would mean day to day. You must rely upon the practices of solitude to make a vow and you must learn. You may read what others have written. You would benefit from discussing the vow with a mentor or your community.

You would then take the vow provisionally, testing for at least six months both the desirability of the vow and the possibility of living with the vow at the center of your life — not as a discipline but as a metamorphosis into one for whom giving up the vow would be inconceivable. You must be radically introspective in the provisional phase. I cannot imagine making a vow, provisional or final, without the benefit of a journal as a mode of introspection leading to prayer.

What is success with a provisional vow? Clarity at the end of the provisional period. Even if you feel the vow is clearly not for you and if this conclusion is authentic — the result of a disciplined effort in self-awareness — you will have achieved a new level of self-awareness.

If you still feel compelled by the vow at the end of the provisional phase, you may make the vow. How this is done? In prayer? In writing? With your partner? With your community? There are processes for the making of vows within religious traditions; no doubt the ceremonial act has importance. But ceremony carries with it the danger of superficiality. The question is whether you have practiced sufficiently to have an entirely new reading of yourself. Therefore, whether there is a ceremony or not, a vow is made and kept in solitude.

Anyone may make a vow. People who are deeply religious, formally or informally; people engaged in therapy or working with a mentor or studying under a teacher; people involved in a twelve-step program or other community; people finding themselves through the practice of solitude — have an advantage in making a vow because introspection and learning are part of their lives.

Loss is a motivator and a setting for avowal. Loss experienced with the benefit of radical introspection brings about humility, which is a kind of self-knowing. A vow can be made at a time of gain, as a vow of charity or service after a financial windfall. A vow can be made in a time of promise and enthusiasm, such as a marriage vow.

One keeps a vow by assessing regularly the progress made in living up to its requirements. When I am anxious or complaisant I look first to my vows and ask myself whether I am backsliding or in some other way falling short of what they require. To ensure that I am not just going through the motions, I turn to my journal. Radical introspection enables me to be aware of what I am doing in relation to what I think I am doing. When I am depressed I invariably find that I have strayed from my vows even though I was sure I was practicing them faithfully.

Keeping a vow opens the unconscious mind, which is repressed as we narrow the frames of our perception to accommodate ourselves to the world. What is found there, especially in dreams, is the true story of one's life. We would prefer to script that story and to some extent we can. But we cannot script the unconscious. Dreams come to us as poems we must make an effort to comprehend. In radical introspection I allow my dreams to teach me about myself.

Vows are dynamic. Keeping a vow of nonviolence may begin by refraining from striking, but as I continue my practice I begin to see that my words can be as violent as my actions. Then I perceive that my soft words can be as violent as my hard ones. Truth requires that my pronouncements be factual, but how many of the social words I speak every day are fabrications? I have found that my vow of truth requires me not to lie outright and to take myself seriously in routine conversation. I have found that even silence can be a fabrication. I have found that supposed truths I have followed for years show up to be false.

A vow requires more and more of the avower, growing as he grows, lifting the bar. As vows become more demanding, they merge. I begin to see that what goes against one vow goes against another. I await the day when all my vows — solitude, truth, nonviolence, service and intended uses — will come together as one.

Vows are demanding and forgiving. No one who makes a vow can live up to its every demand. If one has truly taken a vow breaking it brings on remorse. The absence of remorse when a vow is broken indicates that the vow was not truly taken. Remorse and introspection allow the avower to make amends and return home to a vow.

The practitioner of vows may be Hindu, Buddhist, Jew, Christian, Muslim — a follower of any formal religion or a follower of none. The practice of vows supports and augments religion and aids in the quest for God. Vows do not question teachings but lead to a deeper understanding of religion. The teachings of the exemplars are enigmatic and poetic, inviting introspection and contemplation and making room for vows. The keeping of vows so abstract as solitude, truth, nonviolence, service and intended uses assures the avower of an opening mystical experience while moving him from within toward thought and action consistent with his religion.

Community

My awakening to vows was a later phase of a revelatory process that began for me on a cold night in January nearly a quarter century ago when I visited a meeting of people who described themselves as alcoholics. For that reason alone their organization was unlike any I had known, and it was unique in other ways.

It was not hierarchical. Power belonged to the group, not to ranking individuals. Leadership was considered not in terms of authority but simply as service to the group. Money was hardly mentioned. The group paid its own expenses and made no effort to raise money from outside sources. New members were wanted and welcomed, but there was no advertising for them. The organization did not trumpet its accomplishments; the members followed a tradition of not publicizing anyone's name.

An atmosphere of benevolence and mutual respect prevailed. People spoke to each other thoughtfully. People listened.

Woven into the seriousness of purpose was a lightness of heart and an openness of spirit. People seemed to revel in just being together, as if that was intrinsically significant and somehow enough.

I felt welcomed but not needed. I was suspicious. What did they want from me? I was more comfortable with meetings where people vied for prestige, money or power. I waited for the other shoe to drop.

It never did, at least not in the way I expected. The mystifying difference between this group and others I had known was that people didn't differentiate between wanting for and wanting from. What they wanted for me was what they wanted from me. As I became more involved I realized that my openness to the group's kindness and help was itself the gift I could return. Years later I understood that giving love and receiving love are the same.

My participation in this community led me toward the kind of life in which it was no longer necessary to medicate myself with alcohol to escape the pain of mean-inglessness. I was welcomed into a com-munity founded in loss — everyone there had lost something important — and I began to find my missing self. The group told me in so many words that my finding myself would help them find themselves.

We cannot know what the future would look like in a world where the self is vibrant and the spirit is vital and pervasive. But we can discern principles that would govern our living patterns. Self-realizing human beings would prize their self-realization and would associate in ways that would advance it. The vibrancy of the self as relationship would reverberate in relationships with others, which would enhance self-realizing, which would redound in sounder relationships, and so on in an evolving cycle. The ethos of association in a self-realizing world would be that of community.

By community I do not refer to a city, town, village or neighborhood. I'm talking not about a political entity or an interest group. Community does not refer to characteristics or backgrounds or even political or religious beliefs. Community can grow from affinity but is not defined by it. A group is a community because it shares a principled vision and because the members regard and relate to each other with respect.

Although true community is rare, most of us have been in community at one time or another, in family or friendship, in a school or a religious group, in a military unit or social club. By no means, though, are these automatically communities. It depends on how they envision themselves and how they interrelate.

Many people have had communal experience in an athletic team or an artistic ensemble. Others may recall a business venture or service project in which people listened to each other and spoke directly to get the job done. Maybe the last time you knew community was in your neighborhood as a child or among friends in adolescence. Recollections of such experiences — even though there were imperfections and difficulties — evoke powerful sentiments.

Community requires a commitment — to the shared purpose but also to the coming together, so that the achievement of the purpose and the process of achieving it are inseparable. In community the principles that govern how you play the game converse with the goal of winning. Victory and integrity are inseparable.

The practice of community is fostered in solitude. These things being systemic and cyclical, the practice of solitude is fostered in community. A person raised with the benefit of love who has progressed through the forest of the hero's journey can accept solitude and relish its rewards.

Loving and having been loved, the self-realizing person is self-sufficient within or away from the company of others.

Mentors create relationships in which their love fosters the self-awareness that makes it possible for the person being mentored to perceive and relinquish self-defeating behaviors. Community can be created in psychotherapy, counseling, spiritual guidance and other kinds of rigorous mentorship premised on a mutually committed relationship.

Associations for mutual support such as twelve-step programs are communities for self-building, as are wilderness experiences in which members of the group must support each other to survive. At its best, organized religion provides community.

True community creates a safe haven for respectful self-revelation, self-discovery and discovery of other selves. Social conventions like fashionable attire and small talk have their uses but are insufficient to the formation of community. Community entails a commitment to the quality of interaction that most institutions discourage. Community minimizes hierarchy and bureaucracy. Community attends to process. Like a self-realizing individual, a community is content within itself.

Communities incorporate principle as practice, where the means and the ends merge. The community's integrity becomes the integrity of each individual member. Principle is practiced self-consciously until principle is ingrained in the individual, who contributes it back to the community.

The consistent theme running through community is respect. Respect, the foundation of sustained relationship, is creative. Power can be the basis for short-term relationships, be it political power or celebrity or sex or money. But relationships based on power are unpredictable and do not prosper over time. They depend on fear and they generate fear. They lack intrinsic significance. Power relationships preclude true intimacy because to be intimate is to give up power.

Respect is the opposite of this kind of willful power. Respect emerges from the vibrant self and illuminates the self of the one who is respected. Power talks, respect listens. There is no control in respect. Power gains its power from scarcity and withholding; respect is generous and is premised on the assumption of plenty. Power diminishes, respect empowers.

Respect honors the individuality of the other. Our differences stir up fear. Control seeks to eliminate differences and the risks they create. Respect accepts differences, learns from them and even delights in them.

What happens in community is based on the safety that respect provides. The essential action of respect is attentive, compassionate listening. Listening creates the safe place for an individual to express an opinion, a feeling, an attitude or belief. Respect draws people out of themselves. Respect makes it safe to explore one's own beliefs and to allow new beliefs to form around old topics.

Community does not require its members to be perfect. A group whose members present themselves as perfect is hard-pressed to function as a community. There is no rough edge to accommodate, no shadow to be revealed, no room for weakness, and nothing to tolerate, to learn from or to forgive. Community fosters our learning to love those whose imperfections disappoint us, beginning with ourselves.

What is essential about community is its power to reverse the declining cycle of irresponsibility, opposition and despair. In community the uniting power of love holds its own with the divisive nature of economic and political power. In community we are called upon to let go of power and we are given a safe place in which to do so. In community we discover that in letting go of the power of the world, members acquire the power to reverse the systemic decline.

Where there is a vibrant self there is a soul in search of souls — to embrace, enhance and release. The individual soul is destined to become the soul of another, creating a unity and, in doing so, initiating a chain reaction. More powerful than governments and armies and corporations and foundations, more powerful than logic and science, the soul's ascendancy can reverse the declining cycle of existence.

In a self-realizing society associations that are principally about community, from marriage to education to ethical and religious societies, would provide the collective heavy lifting of the soul.

Human beings explore the outer reaches of their humanity in the interaction of souls; in this interaction there is a transformation — from the life of the child, who defines himself in others, to the life of the adult, self-realizing and self-realized, who can participate in love and experience meaning. This growth happens in the solitary heroic journey and in community.

Conclusion

Every Atom

The young cross their arms, grasp their tee-shirts at the bottom and pull them over their heads to peel them off. How constraining it feels as the shirt bottom and small neck opening pass darkly and tightly over the face! How freeing to pull away the shirt! The world can be grasped as a sweaty, dirty tee-shirt, pulled up over our heads and flung away to reveal a new and limitless reality.

Realizing the self — turning outside in — we are really turning inside out. We emerge from the wilderness into an endless clearing of experience. Here is love and authenticity and meaning and enough. Here is what we seek but lack in our hurried lives. And here is the salvation of humanity. Whether in contemplation of a blade of grass or of galaxies or of the dilemmas of civilization, we bring love's enlightening influence to existence as a whole. To save the world we must grab the world with both hands and pull it over our heads.

I am part of a system and the system is part of me. In every system of which I am part, the system is part of me. I am part of every system. My self, a system, is integrated in my relationships, family, organizations, citizenship, the world of nations, the organic earth, the solar system, the Milky Way, the universe and existence itself.

At a certain point I can no longer identify my role in a particular system because it is remote, but I am there. In what I admire and what I despise, I am there. I cannot associate with anything without associating with everything. I cannot separate from anything without separating from everything. How can I know this?

When self-awareness is attuned, I know. I intuit. I am in sync. I see an eagle flying hundreds of feet above my head and I know the eagle is part of me and I am part of the eagle. I read about the starvation of a child in Africa and I am the mother of that child. I feel love for people I've never met. Someone makes me angry and I want to disown and revile him, but I sense myself in him. I know that I am him. When my self-awareness is low and self-centeredness high, I must take my universality on faith. When I am attuned, I know.

I am present in all systems. My eye peers out of every system and peers in.

What the American poet Walt Whitman wrote in "Song of Myself":

I celebrate myself, and sing myself,
And what I assume you shall assume,
For every atom belonging to me as good
belongs to you.

was not a poetic flight of fancy. To be self-aware is to know intuitively that one is of everything and everything is of one.

The world needs attention and engagement and it needs remaking. I don't mean that it needs overhauling first so we can find fulfillment later when it is a better place. Efforts to re-engineer the world have left devastation in their paths. Certainty and good intention yield misery. This is a hard reality playing itself out on the screen of existence every day.

We perceive that the world needs attention, engagement and remaking when in fact I need attention and engagement, and I need remaking. The idea of saving the world is born of the same blindness that is causing us to destroy the world in fear and anger.

We can be more than rugged individualists, warriors, lawyers, combatants in business and politics; more than problem solvers; more than philanthropists, evangelists and advocates for idealistic causes.

There are moments in life very close to death (though not necessarily close in time) when one realizes that the world does not exist, nor the self, nor even the ideal. Experience of the highest poignancy and clarity gives a momentary foretaste of what lies beyond. The self slips away and there is only unity. In these moments we know limitlessness and feel the welcoming arms of death. We realize that all is well.

Losing the self takes place because of the self, which transcends itself. The whole process is a submission to and a surpassing of the self, a turning inside in order to turn inside out. When we are finally able to begin making that turn, we are well across the arc of life.

We are born in fear and meant to progress to love. Our actions are at first purely pragmatic. We see from birth in terms of physical laws, but within us is the potential to see beyond, in the lawlessness of the spirit. This progression — across the arc of life — is the thing for the human being and the thing for humanity.

How do you change the world? How do you intervene in a system? How do you reverse the devolving cycle of fear that is pressing systems to premature extinction to an ascending spiral fueled by love?

The force of the intangible energy of the self is like a hurricane, sucking up the warm waters of souls into the single energetic flow and releasing them to give life to other selves waiting to grow. The energy of the self realizing itself is irresistible.

Systems die without progression, systems die with progression, nothing is forever. Human beings die from violence and depression; the body falls away also when the spirit has ascended to the highest. Humanity may die in cataclysm or it may live in spiritual ascension, fully accepting the end of days. Which will it be? The essential point is that this is first a question for you and me, the ones wearing the dirty, sweaty tee-shirts.

Can we build selves sufficient to carry the burden of which I speak? Consider the influence of Krishna, Buddha, Moses, Socrates, Jesus and Muhammad, and more recently that of Mahatma Gandhi, Mother Teresa and Martin Luther King, and that of the one who loved you without reserve. And is there a choice? Ascension can be supported by the world but not created by it. Love must come first from the self.

When we think about what exists — from a blade of grass to the architecture of great structures, from the suffering of starving children to the flight of birds, from a joyous family celebration to the workers in the chaos of a factory, from the lover's moistened gaze to the hollow eye of death — we remember the master's admonition, "You must fast."

If reality were placed in a centrifuge and whirled round at ever-increasing velocity, what would be revealed at the speed of light? Gazing out from every atom, the eyeball of the one peering in.

Acknowledgements

Didi Goldenhar edited this book, encouraged me and taught me to trust my words. *Ecology of Being* represents a spiral of collaboration between editor and author. Long may it ascend!

I am grateful to Dorrance and Samuel[*] Hamilton, who provided financial support for the work that laid the foundation for this book. I am grateful also to my friend Peter Scaturro, who made it possible for me to complete the project.

Elizabeth Bailey, Douglas Brown, Bruce Bugbee, Fred Burnham, Randy Fertel, Carol Harris, Jay Hughes, Judy Hutchins, Bob Kiesling, Don Kozusko, David Lynn, Veronica Maldonado, Lynn McAfee, Rebecca McClanahan, Mary Martin Niepold, Fernando del Pino, Paula Robison, Allison Saxe, Peter Scaturro, Julie Teo, John Thornton, Kathleen Waldt, Terry Wallace, John Wannen, John White and Robert Wilson read manuscripts and gave me generous and valuable feedback.

Many people have given me many gifts: my parents, Nancy[*] and Charles White; my sister, Jody White, and my brother, Chuck White; my sons, John and Michael White; their mother, Anne White; lifetime friends Tom Barry, Tony

Canning and Bill Schweitzer; members of the Kenyon College English Department when I was an undergraduate, Robert Daniel[*] and Gerrit Roelofs,[*] and now, David Lynn; friends and partners from law firm days Dick Beckler, Stu Eilers, Leon Jaworski,[*] David Johnson, Alan Levenson,[*] Joe Small, Carl Vogt and Tim Waters; many anonymous mentors and fellow sojourners in recovery from alcoholism; colleagues and friends from Hazelden Foundation Gordon Grimm and Elene Loecher; family therapists Bob Lappin and Maxwell Boverman,[*] who were, and are, crucial to my forming a self; intellectual and spiritual mentors Frederic Burnham and Hilary Hayden; friends, colleagues and clients from International Skye, particularly the faculty of The Summer Institute and the members of Community of Learning; spirit friends in Florida and Montana; friends, colleagues and clients around the world; and all who have permitted me to enter their lives and join them in the quest for meaning.

And I acknowledge and thank especially, with love and respect, John White, teacher, friend, son.

[*]Deceased

Visit us on the Web at
www.ecologyofbeing.com

Gambier, Ohio
New York
2006

$22.95
ISBN 978-0-9777402-0-8
52295>